# Pass
# The
# Test

Observations From a Reluctant Author on
Putting God First, Feeling His Presence, and
Doing the Right Thing in a Complex World

**Chris Kramer**

## *Acknowledgements*

Special thanks to...

My wife, Julie, and my amazing kids, Elle and Will. Your encouragement and love made this possible. I love you immensely.

And thanks to so many others for your advice and encouragement...
Mike, Kirk, Mitch, Burnadette, Lise, Julie, Ken, Mark, Rod, Jim, Jordan, Gus, Scott and so many more of you. Thanks for walking with me in life and encouraging me in this project.

## Table of Contents

## What Others Have To Say...

*"In many ways, Chris Kramer is an ordinary person just like the rest of us: husband, father and successful businessperson. He is extraordinary, on the other hand, in his daily efforts to become a better person by consistently reflecting upon what God wants him to be and become. This book is a "must read" for people who want to improve the quality of their life."*

**~ Ken Smith, District Manager—Central Financial Group**

*"This book provides simple but powerful reminders of how we can interject our faith into our daily life. It doesn't make pie-in-the-sky promises, instead it offers timeless truth that helps us to navigate the big and small decisions we all face, and reminds us that God is with us. Originally, Chris Kramer intended the contents of this book to simply be a gift for his own kids, but I'm sure glad he decided to share it with the world! I know it blessed my socks off, and I'm betting it will do the same for you!"*

**~ Mitch Matthews, Entrepreneur, speaker and best-selling author of IGNITE**

*"This book helps remind you that by making (and keeping) God at the center of your life, you WILL pass all of life's important tests."*

**~ Kirk Johnson, Attorney**

## Foreword

Two men walked side-by-side up a smooth sloped hill to the first tee box at the break of dawn on a sunny Saturday. A gentle breeze, just enough to notice, pushed toward them.

The first man grumbled about hitting into the wind so early in the round, followed by a preemptive complaint about how the hot sun surely would become unbearable by the back nine... and how he'd probably hook one into the woods to start the day.

The second man stood near the same tee box of the same hole at the same time, with the same view, but he saw—and perceived—things differently.

As he took a long slow practice swing with his trusty and familiar oversized driver, he inhaled deeply on the way back, taking in the aroma of freshly cut grass, then exhaled with something close to a whistle to match the rush of Big Bertha, cutting confidently and forcefully through the air.

He could practically taste the joy surrounding him... a

bright and beautiful morning for a round of golf with a curmudgeonly long-time friend. He was filled with optimism that today his Titleist would soar straight and clean and true off his carefully positioned high tee — the sound of titanium meeting urethane, followed by the joy of lifting his eyes from a disciplined head down posture to catch a glimpse of his golf ball soaring so high and deep that it almost disappeared into a coral blue morning sky, before descending safely and playfully onto the middle of a narrow fairway just a soft wedge to the first green.

Both men have the same view. The first man sees flaws and burdens. The second man engages all his senses to soak up and appreciate the moment, discovering joy and meaning in moments that are familiar and far too often overlooked and taken for granted.

The first man uses negativity as a crutch to hide his insecurities and fear. The second man leads with a disarming and almost untouchable optimism that comes not from idealism, but from faith. For him, the darkness is real, but so is the light. And for him, the light wins in the end, and that makes all the difference in the present.

He is alive, created—among other things—to praise his Creator by capturing and perceiving that which the world can no longer see. His eyes are open. Wide.

I submit to you that my friend, Chris Kramer, the author

of the book you now hold in your hands, is the second man. Not to mention... a near world-class golfer.

Enjoy his view. And let it become contagious.

+++
~ *Mike Housholder, Pastor*

## Preface

Originally this book was for my family—especially my children, Elle and Will. I wanted them to know how I viewed the world and what I hoped would be the results of our lives on Earth... for all of us to end up in Heaven together forever.

I wrote this because I want them to remember me and allow me to teach them through this book. I want them to interject God into everything they do because there is never, ever a time when that is not the preferred way to act or think.

I want them to know that we will all screw up, but God will forgive us. I want them to know Jesus Christ is the way and the life. I want them to know they will live joy-filled lives if they turn their lives over to Jesus and that life is so much better when your heart is filled with joy. I want them to know that it is our job in life to further God's kingdom. I want them to know that we will be together forever in Heaven.

Life is short on earth, but eternity is forever. Do your best and make God proud. When you know these things, you will change your heart and often the hearts of those around you.

Most of these writings come from notes I took in

sermons. These teachings led me into what you are about to read. I think everything in life is a test and that when you interject Jesus Christ into the equation, you will pass the test.

You may think of different ways of passing the test than I have written, and that's great because there are many applications for each principle. My goal is for all of us to interject God into the picture so that what we do pleases God. I figure I consider His desires for me into my thoughts about 8% of the time. This is better than before and getting better. Sometimes I do it and am not even aware, which is good because it is where I eventually want to consistently be.

**How This Book Works**
Not every chapter is going to make sense to you or be interesting to you so just move on to the next one as they are all exclusive of one another. What I hope to convey is that interjecting God into your daily tests will help you make better decisions and better influence those around you.

I know that many chapters can sound repetitive and the wording may be somewhat commanding but is that any different than what you read in the Bible or hear in sermons at church?

Sometimes we need to be challenged or hear things in a different way for it to sink in. I hope that the choice of words used in this book does not take away from the main point of interjecting Jesus into every situation in your life.

*Being a Christian is our number 1 job in life.*

Understand that I am not a writer. You'll see that my writings are not perfect. This is something God put on my heart, and, though I fought this feeling for a long time, I finally understood that God was really behind this book.

Read it, enjoy it, and apply it, and it may begin changing your perspective on everything that goes on in your life.

If God puts it on your heart to write a book like this, do it! We are all here to further God's kingdom using the gifts, talents, and blessings He has given us. It might not make sense to you at first, but God is never wrong.

Everything we are and have comes from Him. Now go out and further His kingdom.

**God Bless!**

# Chapter 1

*Trials*

MOST OF US, at some time in our lives, have had low points when we felt alone, scared or hurt. Generally these are fleeting moments, but when that low point lasts for many weeks, or even months, then we have to make a choice to change and look for help.

I went through one of those rough patches, and it lasted for years while I was pursuing my golf career. It had always been my dream to play on the PGA tour, and I was single minded in my efforts. Nothing was going to get in my way. In my infinite wisdom, I cut ties with just about everyone so I could focus completely on golf.

Early on I had great success and was doing even better than I could have imagined. I won events and even qualified to play in a PGA tour event. As can happen, my game went south, and I was going through any money I had—fast.

In this chosen career, back in 1989, it was surprising to me how I could make money or plow through it. For each event, I had to write a check for anywhere from $300-$1000 per tournament. At the end of the tournament, the top 30% would get money back.

At this time, I was playing in at least two of these events a week. This is great if you are playing well, but I wasn't and I went through the cash I'd saved very quickly. To get by financially, I took a night job as a doorman at a nightclub and so began averaging about three hours of sleep a night.

In the third year of my golf pursuit in Florida, I remember spending Christmas alone in a small, rented room in a double-wide trailer that was in desperate need of an insect bomb.

So there I was working two jobs, exhausted, out of money, discouraged, disappointed and friendless. My family was a few thousand miles away. This lasted about four months until I finally decided I needed to come back to Iowa.

I would like to tell you that this is when things turned around, but it wasn't. Even though I was around old friends, many of them were getting married and were moving on to new pursuits. We hung out, but I was always going back to a small, empty apartment. By now I had found a good job and was quite good at it, but I was still very lonely and not living a very inspiring life.

Fast forward to one amazing night when I was introduced to my future wife. This is when I turned the corner a bit because now my life had some purpose. But it wasn't until I got my life on track with Jesus that I felt joy in my heart and understood what was missing in my life. (Don't get me wrong—meeting my wife brought me unbelievable happiness! However, filling the void in my heart that only God can fill made me the man I am today.) I know I am very blessed.

From the beginning of this venture to when I was reacquainted with Jesus Christ my Savior and Lord, it was about eight years. Most of the time I was hurting. I knew I was missing something but I didn't know what it was.

I thought it was a successful golf career. Then I thought it was having money. Then I thought it was finding a great wife. None of these could fill the part of my heart that God filled.

I needed the light to walk to that brought me everlasting joy and answers to what I didn't understand I was missing.

### ~ Pass the Test ~

Life can be hard. Even when you think you are pursuing the right answers, it isn't until you go to the light that you understand that God has the answers your heart is clamoring for.

There is a spot in all of our hearts that is God's.

# Chapter 2

## *No Time Off*

EVERY DAY MATTERS. Every day we can make a difference in someone's life. We all have hundreds of opportunities to make someone's day better. Through nice words, gestures, gifts, whatever it may be we are always in a position to make a difference.

Remember, every day God's Grace is in our lives for our sins. Every one of us receives His Love. Every day matters. Don't throw away a day because you want to be unhappy or feel weighed down. Show Grace and Love to others and do something to make another's day better. We are never alone, and we need to let others know they are not alone either. Do this through words and deeds.

Do not talk down to or try to condemn others because you think they are wrong. Do not be judge and jury of others. Do everything with Love as God does for us.

It is not up to us to force our belief of what it looks like to be a Christian on others. When we do that we only divide the kingdom. Do everything with Love, and give God credit for everything in your life.

Everyone around us should know we are Christians because we do everything with Love and Grace. They may not know right away, but over time, through our actions and words, they will know we are followers of Jesus Christ. When we get good at this, we will find joy in everything we do.

No matter how hard this can be, it will never compare to what Jesus did for us on the cross. He died on the cross for our sins. Never forget. Don't ever forget.

### ~ Pass the Test ~
Don't throw a day away. The attitude you have for yourself and others can make a world of difference. Always show Love and Grace towards those around you and try to make a difference that can improve their day and, hopefully, their life with Jesus Christ.

# Chapter 3

## *He Is With You*

HOW OFTEN DO you have your prayers answered? For me, if I am honest, it has happened thousands of times. What is strange is that I have to try hard to recall them.

I have prayed for help so often that the times all run together. When I reflect, I know God has helped me every time, whether it was healthy kids, protecting me in different situations (like when my snowmobile broke down in a blizzard at age 10 and I was turned around and scared), meeting a woman (my wife) who loves me as much as I love her because I was lonely and lost, or finding meaning in life away from partying, gambling, and other selfish acts to try and make myself happy.

When I follow the voice I hear, I know God is giving me the answer I should follow in every situation. On a daily basis, God guides me and answers my prayers, and, by reflecting, I can recall how God has answered my prayers daily.

Only through my Faith and its growth have I realized what is important in life. God loves me and takes care of me. Only when I began to give God the credit for who I am and where I am today, did I take notice of how blessed I am and that God loves me and takes care of me.

**~ Pass the Test ~**

God is always with us. He hears all our prayers and answers them. Many times the answer is in our minds if we pay attention. Always have Faith and know God brought you to this book right now as a reminder.

# Chapter 4

## *Preparing Kids for Life and Death*

I AM NOT afraid of death. I know that because Jesus Christ died for my sins and ascended into Heaven, I, too, will be with Him in Heaven. God tells us we will spend eternity with Him if we believe this.

My great concern is that my kids, family, friends, colleagues and acquaintances all have this Faith. I know I live a Faithful life, but did I also contribute to those around me in their journey with Jesus Christ so that they have no doubt in their future and impact others' lives as well? I do not want them to mourn my passing but instead feel calmness, warmth and joy in knowing I am waiting for them in Heaven.

Life nor death are to be feared. As a child, I remember worrying about my parents dying. I knew of God but not how life-and-death worked. I was scared because of the unknown and how I would live without them in my life. Nothing ever happened to them, but that fear was still real.

I want my children to be prepared for the ups and downs of life and not live in fear. Even though they may not understand everything right now, they should know that God takes care of them just as He is taking care of me. We will be together throughout eternity.

Through Jesus Christ, we will have all our questions answered. Life-and-death makes sense when we put our

Faith in God. When undesirable things in life happen, turn to God and find peace in Him. It is up to us to never lose Faith and know that life on Earth is short, but eternity is forever.

Realize how blessed you are (Jesus died for our sins so we could be in Heaven forever) and live life with joy. This joy comes from God. Use what God has given you to make a difference in others' lives and help them in their journey with God. Never lose Faith!

### ~ Pass the Test ~
Everything happens for a reason. Some tests are way harder than others. With unwavering Faith we will get through everything. Eventually we will all be together in Heaven, forever.

# Chapter 5

## *Crossroads*

WE OFTEN STRUGGLE with actions we have done or are asked to do by others that we know are wrong. Old friends may want us to participate in activities that originally bonded our friendship, but we know in our journey with God they are not actions we want to participate in any more.

When you are struggling with a choice, I think it is pretty obvious God is talking to you. Be honest with yourself and those around you. When you do what God wants you to do, you will be seen by others the way you know God wants you to be seen.

What defines us is our relationship with Jesus Christ. Help those around you with their relationship in Jesus Christ and encourage kingdom living, and you will find yourself encouraged as well.

Ask yourself these questions. Do I do things in life to make God happy or me happy? What happens when I do everything to make God happy? Do I think I will have a more joy filled life?

### ~ Pass the Test ~
When you hear that voice in your head saying 'pause and consider,' it may be because you're seriously considering the wrong road. God speaks to you and tries to help you in all of your choices. When you choose

right, even when it's tough, you will experience better results and a more joy filled life.

# Chapter 6

## *Upset*

LIFE SPENT WITH God is about recognizing how to turn to Him in all situations in our lives. Everything is a test which can be passed only with God's help and guidance. If you take notice of these occasions more and more each day, you will handle all good and bad times in your life better. This is how you walk with God.

Don't just turn to Him when you need Him. He desires to be the focal point of your life. God desires to have a relationship with every one of us. Every second of every day we have choices to make. How we react to these choices will dictate our moods, feelings, attitudes, personal relationships and how others view us.

To live a Christ-filled life can be hard, but you will be joy filled and will make others' lives around you better. That sounds awfully good.

Why do we choose to be unhappy and want others to know we are upset? Does that make you and others happier or better? We will never be perfect but the more often we can see all the tests in our lives and integrate God, the better our lives will be.

At first it will only happen a few times a week. Over time, if you take a breath, you will recognize God can help you and you will begin to live a better God-filled life.

**~ Pass the Test ~**

Can you name any decision you make that is not wiser when you involve God? The more we interject God into our daily processes and daily decisions, the better the world will be for us and those around us.

# Chapter 7

## *Perspective*

WHY IS IT we can get so excited about upcoming events like sports, concerts, or big community events that only last a few hours but can't get excited about Jesus Christ? Which of these lasts forever? Which one brings you joy forever?

We choose the trivial events because we don't have to think. We are part of a team with others. We don't have to work. This is the dividing line. With God, we need to turn to Him and walk with Him every day. It is work. It is also exciting. I am not saying we should not be excited about special events, but, rather, that we should have perspective.

Events have no lasting effect on our lives, but our relationship with Jesus Christ is forever.


### ~ Pass the Test ~
Have perspective and put Jesus Christ in the right place in your life. Events that we look forward to can be fun and aren't wrong, but Jesus Christ is our pathway to eternal life in Heaven.

# Chapter 8

## *Holy Name*

GOD'S NAME IS holy. It is important that it has meaning every time we hear it or say it.

God is for relationships. God created Heaven and Earth. He is in both places to have a relationship with us. God does not just watch us from a distance. He wants a relationship with us every day. He wants us to have relationships on Earth and Love everyone—including our enemies.

Our Heavenly Father loves us no matter how we are doing. He has His arm around us right now and walks with us at all times. He wants us to find our place in His story.

Adam and Eve had a choice. God told them not to eat from one tree, yet they sinned and chose to eat from it. How often do we choose to sin? Sin is sin, no matter if we do it often or just a few times. We need to realize that even if we are good, it is because of Him, and when we have turned on God, it's only because of His Grace and Love that we are forgiven.

It is easy to see the sin of others, especially for horrible things like murder, but no sin is worse than another. Acknowledging your sin is the first step in having a relationship with God.

We are not perfect and this is why we need a Savior, a

God who never turns his back on us and Loves us unconditionally.

## ~ Pass the Test ~

Because of everything God does for us and because of his son Jesus Christ our Savior and Lord, we must always treat His name as Holy! When we have reverence for the word and name of Our Father in Heaven, it should instantly change our thought process to right over wrong, good over bad and Love and Grace for all.

# Chapter 9

*Not Perfect*

NOT ONE OF us is perfect. There is no perfect person, family or preacher. No one.

In the beginning God created a perfect place, but humans sinned and allowed imperfection to enter the world. Ever since then, God has been trying to show us the way. He has shown us how much, He loves us through His lessons in the Bible and most of all through His son, Jesus, who made the ultimate sacrifice. Jesus died on the cross for our sins, so we can rise up and live in Heaven forever. This is our greatest blessing.

Even though we cannot be perfect, God promises to help us with direction through Grace and Love. God has the power to change us. When we open our eyes and heart, we can see the moments that God is trying to help us. God gives us more than we deserve. If we trust God, we will get more than we deserve.

Often we make God too small. He is the Creator of everything. He knows how many hairs we have on our body. He knows all and has affected our lives in ways for which we will never give Him credit. God's way requires us to trust Him all the time. It takes work, but it will transform us if we let it.

Many times we insist on going our own way, and it usually turns out poorly. When we try to do it on our own, we will always screw things up.

God will always help us if we let Him, so trust God!

When we trust God, He will move in our lives, but we must give Him time while we trust Him. Let go of the need for instant gratification and let Him work. God will provide.

### ~ Pass the Test ~

God is in control. When you trust Him and follow Him, life becomes easier with fewer worries and more joy. Quit believing you control what happens around you, and put your trust in God.

# Chapter 10

## *Take Advantage of Everything God Gives You*

GOD BLESSES US with so much. Often, unfortunately, we wish our time away or don't pay attention to what is happening around us.

With my job, I go to a lot of educational classes. Quite often the classes can be dry, and it's tough to stay engaged. Sometimes I read a paper, leave the room or get up and pace in the back of the room just to get through the class.

When I was asked to speak in front of the class, however, I was pretty nervous and I know I didn't come across very strong so a lot of them tuned me out. I then realized I was not taking advantage of the blessing God had given me to learn during these classes. I realized the speakers were doing their best, are very knowledgeable and that I could learn a lot from them.

Now I always try to give my full attention to the task and learn because everyone is trying their best, and God has information to make me better at my job.

Don't blow off any moments in your life. God is with you, around you and is at all times willing to speak to you and teach you.

### ~ Pass the Test ~

When you realize all moments are tests to improve yourself, you will learn to take advantage and give praise to God. Every moment is a learning moment from God to you.

# Chapter 11

## *Power*

WHEN MOSES LED the Israelites across the Red Sea, he split the water with his staff. He did it through Faith in God and God's power.

What is your staff? Do you have one? Instead of putting our Faith in God, we often turn to things we believe are good luck, which is usually a superstition. We then follow that superstition as long as things go well. You see this in sports a lot. They have no particular reason to believe in their new superstition, but it seems to work for a while.

Life is not easy and moves so fast that sometimes we need to believe something in our lives works for our betterment.

When I play golf, especially in tournaments, I always intend to breathe in the Holy Spirit when I get nervous, but, instead, when I am nervous, I hurry. I completely forget my main intention to put God first.

Superstitions are easy because we implement it and forget about it. It's easy to forget we all have the greatest power source imaginable and often don't turn to Him for His help. Turning to Him might not lead you to victory every time, but it will warm your heart and give you the right frame of mind.

### ~ Pass the Test ~

Turning to God takes consistent attention which is why superstitions are the easy way out. Breathing in the Holy Spirit will become a habit if you put in the effort. God is always there for you, while superstitions only work until they don't.

# Chapter 12

## *Teaching Moment*

DON'T USE GOD'S name in vain. Too often we hear or say "Oh my God."

God's name is Holy and special. Only use it when you want to concentrate on Him. It should be a special time when you're in total sync with God. It should warm you up, calm you down and make you feel good.

When I hear others use God's name incorrectly, it actually does me a favor because it brings me to God for that moment. It also reminds me that this is a sin from the Ten Commandments. It becomes a reinforcing moment for me not to do it myself.

These moments happen daily for me especially when I watch the news. When I hear of all the bad things happening, I instantly determine whether I think it's a good thing or a bad thing. I had to realize that most of the time I'm hearing about sin that goes against the Ten Commandments.

Instead, I can use the news segments to reinforce lessons by attaching a Commandment to each of these bad events. By doing so it brings me back to God, and I'm reminded of His rules.

**~ Pass the Test ~**

By knowing the Ten Commandments, we can learn from everything that we take in around us, consider it through the grid of scripture, and reinforce what God expects from us.

# Chapter 13

*Find Your Places*

DO YOU HAVE a Holy place where you spend one-on-one time with God? As I have attempted to write this book, I have come up against many distractions.

For the longest time I believed that I could do it at home, at work or during relaxing times, but this never worked. I could never give it my full attention.

It finally became apparent that I fully concentrate when I am in the Worship Center at church. When I am there, I feel God's presence and the writing flows like water. I can make it work at home and other places, but it's really an effort to block out everything else and concentrate to be with God.

So, for me, my "go to" place will always be the Worship Center because I can easily relax and be with God. I believe we need to find a place that works for each of us. It takes trial and error, but it is worth it.


**~ Pass the Test ~**
Know the places that work for you and what conditions are needed so you can spend alone time with God.

This is hugely important because alone time and prayer time with Our Father in Heaven is the main way to feel and give your Love to God and to receive it from God. It fills your mind and heart with God's Love.

With that, our life's decisions have meaning and become easier. The guidance, comfort and forgiveness we get from God help to make sense of our lives.

# Chapter 14

## *Focus*

RECENTLY I HEARD a story about a family who was told that mom had two to five years to live. Instead of giving up and doing nothing, they turned to God.

They looked for help from the Church family and they became more Faithful to Christ. The kids became even stronger Christians and in a short time the family put their Faith in God in everything they did.

Miraculously, the mom was cancer free within a year. Months went by only to have the cancer return. This did not dissuade them, nor did they get mad at God.

How many of us could keep the utmost Faith in God when our emotions have been tugged in so many directions?

Currently, the story is happy because she had another clean bill of health. Now, because of Faith, everything has meaning to them, and they have had tremendous influence on many people's lives.

That is what Faith does. It focuses us on what is important and makes the lives of those we come in contact with better. It enriches others' lives and solidifies our Faith in Our Father in Heaven.

**~ Pass the Test ~**
Don't simply go through the motions and let time go by. Focus on what is important. Faith in God should be the most important thing in your life because it not only impacts you but those around you. Start now so you are ready for everything that life throws your way.

# Chapter 15

## *Good Wins*

ALWAYS KNOW THAT God is our judge. He sees everything and knows who has Faith. Even though all of us have sinned, God always allows us to repent.

Good is greater than evil. When you walk with Faith in Jesus Christ, you can always know things will be wonderful because, even if your life here on earth ends, you will continue for eternity in Heaven.

Stay focused on the word of God. Read and learn it. Life is simpler when you follow God's rules and His word. When you wander away and go against His word, it creates an avalanche of problems for you and those around you. To follow with unwavering Faith results in a life everlasting with joy.

### ~ Pass the Test ~

Good wins over evil every time. Make all of your decisions with repentance and a focus on God's word. When you do this in the name of Jesus Christ, with a heart of Love, Faith and Grace, you will be making good decisions.

Chapter 15

# Chapter 16

## *His Gift*

ONLY ONE PERSON ever walked this Earth with perfection and all the answers. Jesus Christ our Savior and Lord is our greatest teacher and example of how to live our lives.

Unfortunately, we all sin, but this can be one of the ways we can learn. Since we are not Jesus, we learn in many different ways. We learn from teaching within the Church, from the Bible, from our parents and teachers, from failures and successes, from life itself and from God. It is up to us to recognize that all situations we are presented with daily are learning situations based upon our thought processes.

How we compute everything that we encounter either reaffirms our Love of Jesus Christ or leads us to unfavorable thoughts or choices. When you put God first, you will have more genuine concern for others. Using the gifts, talents and blessings God gave you to the best of your ability is what God intended. Realizing it is from God is your test.

Often in sports, we see an elite athlete do something incredible and are in awe of their ability. When asked about it, the athlete will tell how hard they worked to get to where they are. While it's true, what we tend to forget is that God gave us these abilities to maximize.

To the credit of that athlete, they are doing more than

most when it comes to doing the most with what God gave them, but usually their motivation is for personal recognition. It is always heartwarming to hear an athlete give credit to God for their success. They understand it is a talent God gave them. The by-product of their success is enjoyment for others.

### ~ Pass the Test ~

We can all learn from every situation in life. It is up to us to pass each test in life by turning to God for the answers and giving Him credit for our successes. We can never be perfect, but by putting our all into what God has gifted us for His credit and the happiness of others, we are passing the test.

# Chapter 17

## *Repent*

SINCE WE DO sin by thought or through action, it is up to us to learn from our sins. When you begin to recognize your sins, you can start to eliminate them. None of us will ever be sinless, but we can minimize our sins and lead better lives.

For me, the sins I struggle with the most are thought patterns I still carry from my past. Many of these thoughts have been ingrained from years of trying to fit in with those I spent time with and I wanted to be accepted by.

It is easy for me to be tempted by things that they have and I don't. It is also easy for me to judge others about how they live their lives, yet since I'm not perfect, I need to leave the judging to the only one who sees and knows all. God knows what is in everyone's heart, and He will be the final judge.

The last several years, I have become much better at recognizing when I sin and because of this I am starting to eliminate some of these thoughts. Because of this, I am learning to become a better Christian.

God loves us and shows us Grace and Love at all times. All He asks from us is that we have Faith in Jesus Christ and repent. Now, for some they think that means they can sin their entire lives and ask for forgiveness on their deathbeds. While this is true, there are a few problems with that logic.

1) Will you have the capacity to repent before you die, or will you die suddenly or be without all your mental activity?

2) By waiting until the end means you miss out on the joy of God's Love which makes life so much better.

3) Life is empty the farther you get away from God's love by continuing in sin.

We have all had problems in our lives which get more complicated by doing things the wrong way. In hindsight we realize that if we had done it the right way the first time, life would have been easier. The same goes for sinning. The less you do it, the easier life is and the more joy you will take in.

### ~ Pass the Test ~

Recognize your sins and repent. The more you do this, the more joy He will bring to you and others through you.

# Chapter 18

## *Photos*

WHAT DO YOU see when you look at a picture of your family? What reaction do you have when you see a picture of a beautiful flower or an amazing sunset? What memories do you have when you hold a cherished memento in your hands that you have kept for years?

Usually these things bring a smile to your face and heart. Normally we feel peaceful and happy. What I've come to realize is that we are recognizing a blessing from God. In our own way, we are thanking Him with that smile or tranquil moment. It seems much like when you give your child a gift, and they are so overjoyed they forget to thank you. At that moment, you don't need your child to thank you because their reaction is thanks enough.

Just writing this chapter brings a smile to my face and opens my eyes to all the blessings around me.


### ~ Pass the Test ~
Look at a special picture as soon as you can. How does it make you feel? Now give God credit for that blessing. How much better do you feel when you realize how much God Loves you? We are so very blessed.

# Chapter 19

*Litter*

How often do you walk by a piece of litter on the ground? Does a voice go off in your head to pick it up?

This happens to me all the time, whether I missed the garbage or someone else did. I used to walk by it if it wasn't my mistake, but now I realize that it is God speaking to me. The Voice says, "Do the right thing."

Doing the right thing is always right. Getting mad about it and turning my back on the problem is the wrong response.

These types of things happen frequently, and though we often think it is not our problem, it is. Listen to the Voice and pass the test. In our house we talk of two things, make God proud and do your best.

When you have Love in your heart, passing these tests becomes easier and easier.


### ~ Pass the Test ~
Listen to God and you'll have the strength to do the right thing. Even if no one sees you, God knows. He always knows what you are thinking and what is in your heart.

# Chapter 20

## *Dark Times*

DARK TIMES HAVE taken over the United States of America. God has been pushed to the side and a false God is now worshiped. Government is one of the false gods of almost 50% of Americans.

Apathy, contentment, hatred, jealousy and envy have also become the norm. Helplessness is a common theme. The Ten Commandments have been thrown aside as selfishness has become the prevalent way of thinking. It is hard for me to see a rosy picture when I see all the things I love being destroyed.

So what to do? Do I mope around and try to figure out what I should do to make my life better? Should I give up and just be sad and complain? Should I continue to explain how godless our society has turned and how the country is destroying itself?

Well, I needed to wake up and stop complaining! There is and always has been one answer—God! Our country was created under God and He blessed us.

Like other societies before us, we have become lazy and content with how blessed we are, and we have stopped putting God first. Statistics show that Americans are turning away from God more and more each year.

Government is pushing Christian values away and siding with atheists. It looks and sounds bad. But now the good news! God is with us and never leaves our side. He still performs miracles in our lives and blesses us every second of every day (think Jesus). God's Love is unconditional, and we are forgiven if we repent and turn to Him. God is embedded in our hearts, and when we were pressed, we temporarily turned to Him.

On 9/12/01 and for months later, our country filled Churches across the country, because we knew He was our only chance to recover. Proof that we know where to turn when looking for answers.

We must remember this because our country can turn around, and it can happen rather quickly. The question is whether we are willing to put in the work and effort needed to participate in turning things around.

Are we willing to give up the parts of our lives that make things comfortable? Personally, if I reflect, there are many things I can give up in an effort to change my life. Currently, I work, watch TV, spend as much time with my family as possible and enjoy a lot of good things in life.

I live a nice middle class life with a few extras like following our favorite college athletics, golfing, watching TV, playing games, watching movies, and doing what we want when we want to (freedom). I go to Church and spend time improving my relationship with God every week, but I spend considerably less time doing that than I do with the diversions in my life.

I believe this is probably the way most of us are. We put the diversions first and only spend time with God when it is convenient. Is it any wonder that our society has pushed God aside and a godless society has risen?

Here is what we have to do to change to create a society that is stronger than ever. Remember, God is with us but it starts with each of us individually.

We must put God first and from there, watch it spread outward. It's time to work to change our society's lax attitude towards Jesus Christ Our Savior and Lord.

Here is a checklist for passing God's test:

1.  Quit being selfish.
2.  Tithe. It is all God's anyway. It's just our way of proving to God we know it.
3.  Strengthen your Faith.
    - Spend a lot more time in the Bible and with the church.
    - Put God first.
    - Strengthen your heart with Faith.
4.  With everything you do, give Jesus the credit outwardly.
    - Finish each deed by blessing someone in Christ's name.
    - Pray for others.
    - Wear God on your sleeve and don't hide your Faith.
    - Make it a habit to give Christ Jesus the credit for everything verbally.
5.  Allocate wasted time to helping others. It's easy to indulge in too many pleasures that could be redirected to the community around us.
6.  Obey the Ten Commandments. These Commandments are from God. Do not allow for any gray areas.
7.  Be a leader, and do everything with Love and

Grace like God does for us every day.

8.  Teach your kids and grandkids about your Faith and what is truly important. God answers all our worries and questions.
9.  Meditate and pray to God for guidance. Follow His dream for you.
10. Never give up.

### ~ Pass the Test ~

I believe we have taken too much for granted and lived rather easy lives. Because of this, we have marginalized God. We need to step up and be leaders in our communities with unwavering Faith in Jesus Christ Our Savior and Lord.

We must get involved and speak of Jesus Christ in everything we do. When we do things out of Love, it has great potential to change hearts. It will not be easy, and it will take a lot of sacrifice, but it must be done in order to be a part of God's work in people's lives. Wear the shield of God in everything you do.

Having Faith in God will not solve our problems in society. We must act. He gave each of us gifts, talents and blessings to help others, and we must do it if we are to further God's kingdom.

# Chapter 21

## *Worrying*

LIFE WILL NOT seem fair a lot of the time, but having a relationship with God helps us get through all of the problems in our lives. Without Faith in God, we may be mad, unhappy, a worrier or vengeful and just plain lost. With God, we know that everything is a test of our Faith, and, in the end, we spend eternity in Heaven with Him.

We have choices every day on how we approach everything that happens to us. We learn from adversity. In sports the only way to get better is to learn. We learn from losing, pushing ourselves past what we thought was possible, from practicing, attitude and trial and error. If all we had to do was show up and be crowned the winner at everything we tried, we wouldn't learn a thing.

The great thing about athletics is that there is a winner and a loser and how we handle both of these is a test of our Faith. For the winners, knowing God gave you the talents and giving credit to God for these talents is a part of your test. For those who lost, knowing God loves you, has blessed you and is the most important thing in your life puts perspective into the activity.

### ~ Pass the Test ~

Our Faith will be tested throughout our lives. For those who study the Bible and know God is with them always and that Jesus Christ died for their sins, life becomes less about worries and more about perspective of our final destination. Make your life, and the lives of those around you, better with God's Love.

# Chapter 22

## *Challenge*

I DON'T KNOW about you, but when I think about God, Jesus Christ or the Holy Spirit, I feel better. When someone makes his Faith be known, I feel better. When someone blesses me, I feel better. When someone prays for me, I feel better. Our challenge with everyone we meet is to either greet or finish our interaction with a blessing.

When we say goodbye to someone we might finish by saying:

1. God bless you
2. Peace be with you
3. Have a blessed day
4. Have a Faith filled day
5. God Loves you
6. May the Holy Spirit fill you up
7. Walk with Jesus

Studies show that when we think positively, we will do better at our activities. What is more positive than realizing how blessed we are? Share it with others and make their day better as well. This way we not only help someone else's attitude, but our own as well.

**~ Pass the Test ~**
Be bold in living your Christian ways. At the very least, you will feel better and who knows--you may make

someone else have a better day as well.

# Chapter 23

## *Follow the Ten Commandments*

WE ALL KNOW the difference between right and wrong. This is because of God's Ten Commandments.

We live in a world filled with lies and half-truths being told by our President, politicians, the press, and those around us for self-serving motives and done without regret. Be strong enough to do the right thing. Stop bending God's rules. This is how our country has become so dark.

Quit voting for politicians who blatantly stand against God's rules. No one is perfect, but when a politician's platform is based upon man's rules or mob rules, we need to stand up for what is right. It doesn't matter if you're a lone wolf—do the right thing. No justification can make an immoral stance right.

It is also our job as Christians to pray for those who have turned away from God. We need to be leaders. Even though they may cause us pain and heartache, as Christians we know we are all God's children, and everyone has an opportunity to repent and be part of God's kingdom in Heaven.

### ~ Pass the Test ~

Do the right thing. Know the Ten Commandments and follow them. We must follow them, without exception, for they are the word of God. He did not leave any gray areas. Remember, God knows everything you do and what is in your heart.

# Chapter 24

## *Teach Kids*

WE LIVE IN a world where kids' successes are a first priority for many families. Striving to be the best is at the forefront of all activities. Parents have their kids spend most of their time practicing and competing. In sports, this has become the norm.

We don't let kids be kids anymore. Worse yet, we teach our kids bad baseline attributes that they will carry with them through life. There is a reason we call these the formative years--because kids form their habits and thoughts in their early years.

A few of the lessons I see being taught to our kids right now:

1.  Win at all costs
2.  Try harder and you will win
3.  You can do better
4.  You did something wrong
5.  The activity is more important than your Love
6.  Nothing is as important as the activity
7.  Something isn't fair
8.  It is not your fault
9.  It is okay to get mad
10. It is okay to act irrationally (parents this may be you)

Sports and other activities are good and they do teach some lessons for life, but none of this is more important than having Jesus Christ Our Savior and Lord as our foundation for all of life. When we have this priority first, kids learn to handle adversity.

We will all go through adversity and trying times, and we all need to know the difference between right and wrong. How we handle this is based upon our Christian values. Joy comes from Faith in God. Happiness is a fleeting moment. Joy warms our hearts and can be with us forever when we realize how blessed we are.

When I tried to make it as a professional golfer I practiced as much as humanly possible. Generally, most of the golf round is spent around the short game which is on the greens or near them. Approximately 50% of the game is putting. Do you think I spent 50% on practicing putting? No. Instead I wanted the perfect swing. I didn't put the time into the foundation of the game where winning and losing generally happens.

In life, our foundation is in Jesus Christ. I think my first priority in teaching my kids should be demonstrating and explaining this. Nothing is more important than having a relationship with God.

### ~ Pass the Test ~
Have your priorities straight and have them straight for your kids. Do not sacrifice your kids' foundations for fleeting happiness. Put learning about God and spending time with the church first at all times. Our kids will live better lives if we do.

# Chapter 25

## *He Knows*

HUMANS LOOK AT outward appearances.

God looks at our hearts.

God only cares about our hearts. He knows our every intention, and He knows if we do things for Him or ourselves. He knows if our actions are based on Love or selfishness. He knows if we care more about what others think about us or what He thinks about us.

Our media is full of following the attractive people in the world. Most shows and stories are filled with media anointed stars. Gossip about these people fills up hours of coverage in our lives every day. We are led to believe we should be more like them in the way we look and act. Do you fall into that trap?

When we care more about what others think of us than what God thinks of us, we will be tempted to make bad decisions. God gave each of us different looks, talents, gifts and blessings. He loves each of us equally. He only cares what is in our hearts. If we live life to make Him proud, without a need for recognition from others, we can make a positive difference in this world and help others.

Life on Earth is about using what God gave us to make others' lives better in their journey to Heaven. In doing so, it is also our job on Earth to do everything for the glory of God and give Him credit outwardly.

### ~ Pass the Test ~

Remember, God knows our hearts at all times. Make Him proud and go through life to make Him proud. If we do, we will live a fulfilled and complete life on Earth. We will make a difference in others' lives and will have helped further God's kingdom.

# Chapter 26

*Choosing a Team*

RECENTLY, I WAS talking with friends about who our favorite professional sports teams are. Iowa isn't home to any professional organization, so growing up we don't really have a team that we're prone to love. We tend to choose our favorite teams based upon who is winning when we are introduced to those sports as kids.

For me, my favorite teams were the Miami Dolphins (Super Bowl champs that year) and the Boston Red Sox (beat out the Yankees for the division and had a memorable World Series). The same has happened with my son. As I've watched him grow up, he has enjoyed rooting for the teams that are winning. We want to be on the winning team. To support these teams I own hats and t-shirts with their names on them. These are seasonal teams.

I also choose to be on God's team. This is not a seasonal team but year round.

In the past, I chose to go with the crowd, and we made some bad choices (now granted, this is not a team but in a general sense it works like a team). We definitely did not win all the time, and we got in trouble at times. This still happens today with choices we make as to how we act.

Often we choose to go with the crowd, whether it is

drinking, using poor language, telling stories, belief systems or just acting badly. This was a hard lesson for me to overcome and for the most part I have, but it can be easy to join the crowd and do dumb things.

### ~ Pass the Test ~

It is never too late to choose to be on God's team. His team never loses. He wins out over everything. That alone should be an automatic draw for most of us because we love being on the winning team.

What is even greater is that God's team will accept us at any time and forgive us for all our screw-ups the second we join.

# Chapter 27

## *Why Wait?*

EVERYONE CAN TURN to God and follow Jesus Christ at any time and be saved for eternity. People will say then why don't I wait until my deathbed? What they miss is walking with Jesus. He makes life so much better, and the sooner you follow Him the more you'll truly enjoy life and live it with joy.

What makes you happier? Giving a present or getting one? To me this is the difference between joy and happiness. Receiving a gift brings me happiness while giving a well-received gift warms my heart and fills me with joy.

We all have the opportunity to partake in God's warmth and live joy filled lives. You can start today. For me, once I put others' lives before my own, it helped me become calmer, happier and more rational, and I experienced more Love. I started to have a glimpse of how God sees each of us. God made all of us for a reason, and even though we are all different, we each have a purpose that God thinks is special.

Try to see others through God's eyes. When we do, we become less reactionary and judgmental, and we can genuinely extend Love and Grace to all.

**~ Pass the Test ~**
Don't miss that which is around you. Life is so much

fuller when we follow God's ways. Living in darkness and selfishness deprives us of a life filled with Love from God. Pray to God that you see the world through His eyes.

# Chapter 28

*Celebrate Every Day*

I REALLY ENJOY the time between Thanksgiving and Christmas. Listening to the music, enjoying the season, watching the shows--they all make me feel great. Even though my kids are too old for some shows, we still enjoy watching The Grinch Who Stole Christmas. The message you get from the show is tremendous. It is a great reminder of what Christmas is about and why we celebrate it.

In today's culture, we put the food and presents ahead of the meaning and reason for Christmas. In the show, even though the Who's lost everything, they still awakened with unwavering spirit and celebrated the true meaning of Christmas. They did it with joy in their hearts.

How are you doing with Christmas? Do you grow with excitement because it is when you celebrate the birth of your Savior and Lord, or do you grow in contempt, anxiety and worry about how it affects you?

Now, how do we approach every day? Instead of dreading the coming day or week, shouldn't we celebrate each and every day because of Jesus Christ? We should recognize how blessed we are every day no matter if we are rich with possessions or wearing the same clothes as the day before.

## ~ Pass the Test ~

Each day is a blessing because of Jesus Christ, Our Savior and Lord. It doesn't matter if it is December 25 or June 12, we should all celebrate each day and not be overtaken by our material goods. Make the most of each day and give praise to Jesus Christ.

# Chapter 29

## *Turn to God*

WHAT DO YOU believe God is capable of? Be honest. Is your God the one who created the Heavens and Earth and parted the Red Sea? Or is God just someone you turn to when you need help?

If God is who created everything in our lives and in this world, then is He capable of making our lives better every day? If we walk with God, should we let humans around us tell us what makes our lives better? The world around us tells us how we should think and what is right and wrong, yet we all know deep down something is wrong. I believe this is why our country is so unhappy.

If we are looking for true happiness then we should walk hand-in-hand with Jesus Christ. He, rather than the world around us, has the answers for our life's questions.

If God is capable of creating everything in our lives, I believe He can uncomplicate our lives here on Earth. It takes commitment and 100% of our hearts, but our lives will never be the same again. We will know true joy.


**~ Pass the Test ~**
Do you believe the world around you truly knows what is best, or do you trust your Creator? What can go wrong when you put all your Faith in Jesus Christ, Our

Savior and Lord? By doing so, your eternal life will be spent in Heaven forever.

# Chapter 30

## *Put Him First*

I AM A dad, and I want to protect my kids in every way possible. I know I can't be with them 24 hours a day, so I try to teach them how to process every situation.

When I look back, I realize kids learn almost everything from the way I, as a parent, talk and act. Kids see and hear everything. So, if I try to teach them lessons but turn around and do the opposite, they will learn to do what they see me do.

Since I'm not perfect, my kids will see me when I sin. How I react after sinning is one of the ways I teach them the difference between right and wrong.

As a parent, teaching our kids how to consistently make Christ-based decisions will teach them the difference between right and wrong. How we know what is right and what is wrong is rooted in The Ten Commandments and our understanding of Faith.

As parents, helping our kids understand the Bible and putting God first in our lives is the only way to teach our children. To do so, we ourselves must do the same. This is the hard part. The old saying "do as I say not as I do" doesn't work because our kids see and hear everything, and they want to emulate us.

There is no way to be a perfect parent. Introducing our kids to the Creator of the Heavens and the Earth and the only perfect human to walk the Earth is the best way to lay a foundation for our kids to process the world. The more intimately kids know Jesus Christ, the better decisions they will make.

We, as parents, cannot teach our kids how to react to every situation, but God can. If our kids know to put Him first, they will be in a stronger situation every time.

### ~ Pass the Test ~

Turn to God. Right and wrong come from God. Knowing, living, and teaching this to our kids is the best way to equip them for life. When they understand this and know God is with them at all times, the better their choices.

# Chapter 31

## *Seek Out God's Dream for You*

THROUGHOUT MY LIFE I have had many dreams. The one I pursued for many years was trying to become a world-class golfer. God blessed me with talent to play golf. From age two, I had a golf club in my hands and spent countless hours practicing and playing. For several years I played as a professional and even was blessed to have the opportunity to play in a PGA tour event.

At the height of my pursuit of a golf career, I practiced a minimum of 12 hours a day. I made sacrifices as well. Namely, taking on life by myself. I became a loner so that I would not be distracted from my end goal. I can honestly look back and say I gave it everything I had and was pretty close, but it was not to be. At first, I was sad that it didn't work out, but now I look back and realize it made me the stronger person I am today.

One thing that became very obvious to me was that I was pursuing my dream. I never turned to God nor asked Him what His dream was for me. I went after what I wanted and not what God wanted me to do. Golf was not meant to be the pedestal I would use to help others.

I finally turned to God for His dreams for me. He put this book on my heart, and, as you can probably tell, I am not a professional writer. I rebelled against God at first. As time went by, the feeling in my heart got stronger and I finally succumbed to His dream. God will lead you if you let Him. Don't be afraid. God will give you everything you need to succeed.


### ~ Pass the Test ~

Pray to God for His dreams for you. His vision and your own heart will become clearer to you through constant prayer. If you are not sure if it is His dream for you, you will know in your heart because it will be something that helps others and you can do it in the name of Jesus Christ. Turn to Him and He will lead you.

# Chapter 32

## *Temptations*

WE ALL FANTASIZE about things we wish we had, skills we could use or groups we wish we could be part of. We dream of having different lives than what we currently experience.

Many of the tests we have are opportunities to live differently rather than doing what others are doing. However, sometimes we justify going down roads we shouldn't. Later we try and cover up our mistakes so the sins we committed will hopefully just go away.

Don't let temptations take over your life. Stay away from the temptations, and you will be less likely to sin.

One of the biggest temptations we have thrown in our faces is sex. It is promoted in every aspect of our lives from TV, to magazines, to the way everyone dresses.

This is just one of the many temptations which have resulted from our culture not living in the fear of God. When we know that God watches our every move and would be disappointed in what we are doing, we will be less likely to pursue activities He would not approve of.

### ~ Pass the Test ~

God knows everything we do. Temptations are obvious tests, but if we live in the fear of God and don't want to disappoint Him, we will make better decisions. Failing these tests are sins that usually grow to create devastating problems for many people in our lives. Live to please God, and we will receive his blessing.

# Chapter 33

## *The Cross*

WHEN YOU ARRIVE at Church, do you get rid of your troubles and listen to God? Can you put away your troubles while you are with the Church?

If you can't, then stop and look at the cross and remember that Jesus Christ died on the cross for your sins. For you He died and because of this, you are blessed. Realize no matter what is going on in your life, you are blessed.

You don't have to be in Church to remember what Jesus Christ's life means to you. Consider starting a new thing in your life today. Look around and find the reminders around you. When you try, you can find a cross in everything you see.

In the areas you spend a lot of time, put items around you that will remind you of Jesus Christ. When you remind yourself how blessed you are because of Jesus Christ Our Savior and Lord, you will begin to have a better perspective. The more you can do this, the more your heart will fill with Love.

### ~ Pass the Test ~
Seek out the crosses around you. They are everywhere at all times. You are blessed!

# Chapter 34

## *Flying*

I HAVE LIVED with a fear of flying my whole life. Now when I fly, I pray for the plane, crew, pilot, other planes, weather, air traffic controllers and our safe passage to our destination. This helps, but what helped me the most was when I realized that I would never know if we had an accident—at least not on earth. I would know by my new destination.

When I give everything to God, I realize He is in control of all the events in my life. I shouldn't worry about things (like death) that I can't control. I will put my Faith in Jesus Christ.

It shouldn't take events like flying for me to have my affairs in order with God. I should always have Faith in Jesus and put Him first at all times because anything could happen to me.

**~ Pass the Test ~**
When you have Faith in Jesus Christ and put Him at the forefront of your day, you can live a worry free life that is in the hands of God.

# Chapter 35

## *How to Handle Winning*

NONE OF US wins every time. Whether it is our own sport, an individual or a team we support, we will all encounter losing. Because of this, it is important to know how God wants us to act when we, personally, or our favorite teams are blessed with accomplishments.

Winning comes from God who blessed us (or the teams we follow), with gifts and talents to accomplish these feats. When we are blessed with winning, acknowledging God for the victory is not only good for us but sets the example for others. Even though winning is fun, it is only a moment in time and making God proud is still always our lifelong goal.

It is a very lonely, and eventually a very scary way to go through life if we act poorly when we do well and believe it is 100% our doing. Remember, we will all encounter both winning and losing. To treat others like we want to be treated is always a great rule of thumb.

Be proud of your accomplishments, but give credit where it is due. Know that putting God first will prepare us for all of the results we live through. Give every day and everything you do your best effort. When God blesses you with victories, be humble.

## ~ Pass the Test ~

Winning is a test in understanding how blessed we are and knowing from where the blessings come. Sure, we may work hard or our favorite team may do well, but knowing that God is in charge should humble us.

As quickly as being happy with success may come, it may all go away. The only joy we can truly have comes from our Faith in Jesus Christ, Our Savior and Lord, who died on the cross so we may be in Heaven throughout eternity.

# Chapter 36

## *Handling Losing*

WE WILL ALL have days in which we don't do well, or our favorite teams struggle.

It is so easy to get mad or frustrated in disappointing results. What we need to realize is that losing is yet another test of our Faith in God. How we handle it is very important.

Too often we think bad luck or unfair conditions dictated our circumstances. When in truth, if we gave our best effort, we realize someone had to win and someone had to lose. If we believe we could have done better, it is a problem we must resolve. If we believe others caused us to lose, then we are not handling adversity very well.

The best learning we will ever endure is through losing. We find out what was needed to win and what changes we need to make.

All competition is, in a way, a diversion from life. The only way to truly win is to never lose Faith in Jesus Christ. Through Him, eternity is guaranteed in Heaven.

### ~ Pass the Test ~
How we handle and learn from losing is the barometer of our Faith in Jesus Christ. Losing is a tough test, but it's only a test. We all win in Jesus Christ.

# Chapter 37

*Praying*

DON'T FOLLOW RULES or preconceived ways to act when praying (talking) with God. Be open with Him. He can handle it. The Lord's Prayer teaches us to pray.

God is with us all the time. He listens to what we say to Him, and He does care about what we're going through. Jesus had many rough times, but He always knew what life on Earth was about for Him and, also, what things lie ahead for us here on earth.

We will all have good and bad days. God is there to listen, and He will guide our minds and hearts. In many of the Psalms, David cries out to God and, though his circumstances often don't change, God works on his heart. For me, just talking with Him and knowing He is listening makes every situation bearable.

He may not always answer my prayers the way I want, and those tests in life are very, very difficult. Knowing He loves me and that I will be with Him throughout eternity still means more than any problem I can have on Earth. Besides, whom should I turn to other than the Creator of Heaven and Earth. Through Him, anything is possible.

## ~ Pass the Test ~
Pray to God at all times. He cares, and He is with us and is working through us all the time.

# Chapter 38

## *Never Rest*

WE ALL HAVE highs and lows in life. Thankfully, God is constant.

In my Bible study group, we were giving thanks for all that we have been blessed with this past year. For me, I realized I'd grown a lot and been blessed with so much over the year. This happened with every guy in our group as we each gave thanks.

One gentleman in our group was uncharacteristically quiet. He is our biblical scholar and the rock of our group. He said things were not going well for him. This never happens with him. It made me realize that even though I am filled with joy and my life is free of extreme trials right now, there are always people who are hurting. There are always people who need my help through prayer and action.

Don't take a break from God, life and others when your life is going through a time of respite or recent problems have been resolved. God wants us to use our commitment to Him and blessings from Him to stay active in others' lives and lift them up.

### ~ Pass the Test ~

We are all blessed whether we're enduring times of hardship or experiencing more restful phases. When life is going well, make sure you are helping others and checking on those you know because they may need your help. Also, remember that there are people who can help you when you are suffering.

# Chapter 39

*Emergency Room*

As I WRITE this, I am sitting in an emergency room. About nine hours ago, I clumsily got my foot caught on the steps and trapped them under my body as I was carrying a Christmas gift down the stairs. I was proudly taking it to the tree because I really felt like I had a great gift for my wife. I didn't want to break it so I saved the gift and hurt my ankle or Achilles heel. As the day went on, I couldn't walk on my foot so my wife thought it best to get some experts to look at it.

When I arrived at the hospital, there were four people and one big emergency ahead of me. In the waiting room were two really sick gentleman. One had a broken arm and the other an ankle injury. Soon after, a baby came in and was very sick and needed attention. It was going to be a long night.

Because my pain was not horrible, I had the right frame of mind to handle the wait. I felt like a wimp when I looked at how terrible everyone felt. I tried something new and began a conversation with the wife of one of the ill gentleman and talked about my Faith.

The lady went on to tell me she is the daughter and granddaughter of pastors. She grew up attending church regularly. She is the mother of three young girls, and her life had not been easy. Her past included a divorce, and, most recently, a daughter who almost died and had been in the hospital for weeks. During all her troubles, she lost her way and quit fellowshipping with other believers.

We talked about Christmas services at *Lutheran Church of Hope* (the church I attend) and she mentioned how she had just thought about attending again. Throughout this hour-long talk, she cried quite often and recalled how important her Faith was to her and how she wants her girls to have it as well. She began to glow with anticipation as this revelation occurred.

The other gentleman, who was very sick himself, chimed in about how *Lutheran Church of Hope* had made a huge difference in his life. He was about 40 years old and had had a very tough life. He'd had a heart attack and four types of cancer throughout his life and still he didn't complain.

My impression of the night is that the lady I spoke with and her family will be attending church regularly now. It really made an impression on her hearing from advocates about how wonderful God is.

See why I feel like a wimp with my ankle problem? However, God had a purpose for me tonight. This night is not about me, and sometimes I need to be reminded that life is about helping others in their journey with God.

### ~ Pass the Test ~
Do not keep Jesus Christ to yourself. It shouldn't have taken being trapped in a small room, with everyone feeling poorly, to have brought this out. Share your Faith in Jesus Christ with others, and you'll be amazed at the results.

# Chapter 40

*Attitude Matters*

I MADE A discovery recently about being a servant in less than desirable circumstances. My wife and I attend a Christmas party every year with several other couples. This party used to be the highlight of the year, but it has lost a little luster in recent years. The bands that have played for us the last few years have not been as much fun, which has resulted in the crowd not participating at a high level.

What used to be a very interactive night has become a night when we tend to sit around. This year, however, I remembered why I go to this event. It is one of the few nights when my beautiful wife gets all decked out in fancy clothes. She glows, and I love it. When you have young kids, nights like this are few and far between and needed.

This year's band was probably the worst one to play for us in eight years of going, yet my wife and I danced all night long and had a great time. The only thing that really changed was my attitude. I stayed positive and, though I am not a great dancer by any means, I don't think a soul noticed.

### ~ Pass the Test ~

Life is what we make of it. Making someone you Love happy, by keeping a great attitude, can make a nondescript night into a memorable night. God gave us the ability to serve others in any circumstance.

# Chapter 41

## *Appreciation/Competition*

I REALLY LIKE athletics, and I especially like the competition. Whether I'm participating, my child, a friend, or my favorite team is, it is fun to be involved. During competition I was tested in many ways.

For me, each of these situations provided me with a different test, but the same answer. Unfortunately, though, it took me until I was 46 to understand the answer, and I still don't get it right all the time. I now have a better understanding.

*First situation, I am competing.*

A few of the tests I encounter are nervousness, confidence, disappointment, and elation.

*Second situation, someone I care about is competing.*

The tests I encounter during these events are nervousness, commentary on how it could go better, caring too much, happiness or dealing with undesired result.

*Third situation, my favorite team is competing.*

The tests I encounter here are anticipation, (which results in me pushing things to the side including time with God) and lots of commentary. I think I have all the answers and that my great analysis will change the outcome of the game (which of course it won't). It will be either a win or loss both of which present challenges on how I handle the result

The answer to handle all of these situations? Appreciation.

Competition is not only a test to see how we compare to others, but, more importantly, an acknowledgment that it is a diversion in our life that God blessed us with. It is not meant to be a diversion from God. When we interject God into each of these competitions, we will appreciate the moment in time.

### ~ Pass the Test ~

The next time there is a competition, stop and write down all the blessings involved with that event. You will be amazed at how many you recognize. This will give you an appreciation for what you are about to be involved.

Competition can severely test our Christianity, but when we open our eyes and appreciate how God is blessing us, we can react as Christians and appreciate God's Love.

# Chapter 42

## *Most Fears are the Opposite of Faith*

I HAVE THIS problem with having images go through my mind of what might happen in situations. One of the worst is my fear of heights. When I am up high, I have flashes go through my mind that a railing might give way or I might somehow fall over an edge, plummeting to my death. This fear of heights is a lack of Faith in God. Of course, I am not writing about being dumb about this fear and testing my Faith by walking on a ledge but day-to-day fear that is irrational because the structure I am on is known to be safe.

If I look out the window of a hotel room, the floor isn't going to buckle nor will a window magically open that I will fall through. Yet this is what I fear when I get close to upper floor windows. This is a lack of Faith in God. It applies to all fears, rational or irrational.

When I fly I have to have Faith in God that I will arrive safely. Fear of not being safe is to think God is not in control. I have heard of plane crashes and bad things happening in life, but when I have unconditional Faith, I know that if the worst thing actually happens, I will be with God. That is what Faith is all about, having Faith in Jesus Christ and spending eternity with Him in Heaven. If God decides He wants me in Heaven now, He knows best and I will be in Heaven.

### ~ Pass the Test ~

When you have fears, it means you don't trust God. This doesn't mean you put God to a test, but, rather, leave it to God to decide your fate. When you have unwavering Faith in Him, you don't have to worry about the outcomes in daily life because He is with you in life and death.

# Chapter 43

## Government is not God

THE UNITED STATES has been heading down a road that, I believe, is leading to its destruction. Our government has been injecting itself as the problem solver to all problems. Whenever anything happens (good or bad), our government has an opinion as to how we should think and act.

Turn on the TV news and we will nearly always hear a piece about our federal government commenting or complaining about something that is happening. The problem, as I see it, is that if they can identify a problem, they can feel free to use their power to intervene (or interfere) and try to solve it.

Obviously, our government provides services and laws we need, but by and large, they are not needed if we are following Jesus Christ.

Where do you turn if you perceive something to be wrong? Do you have a support system you believe in? Do you have unwavering Faith in God?

When our country was established, our founding fathers put their Faith in God. George Washington made a covenant with God to bless our country as long as we put Him first in our lives and realized everything we have comes from Him. In that day, laws were written after reading Scripture and with God in mind.

Laws were to be written so everyone could understand them. If the written laws were too lengthy to be understood or comprehended, they didn't pass because all of God's people needed to be able to comprehend them. Look at God's Commandments. They are perfectly understandable.

Imagine if our government leaders put Jesus Christ first to help them come up with their solutions. I think we would be better off as a society. I also believe it is up to us as individuals to have unconditional Faith in God and create our own local support system to help us.

Church, neighbors, and community are there for us to turn to when we need help. When we have this, we won't need someone in Washington, DC to fix our problem. I encourage you to find and be a part of a support system. I've been fortunate to find mine in West Des Moines, IA.

### ~ Pass the Test ~

Everything comes from God. He is God and not those in Washington, DC. The right answers come from God so put Him first in your life.

# Chapter 44

## *What Is at the Top?*

WHAT IS THE most important thing in your life? What would you like to be the best at? What makes you special?

If you were going to make an accomplishment tree, what would be at the top as the most important? Do you dream of wanting to be the best at something? It could be sports, academics, being a parent—anything at which you hope to excel.

Where does God fit into your story? Answer it honestly and then answer this. Of all your dreams, wishes, and goals, which will last throughout eternity?

If God is at the top of your tree, do you put Him first at all times? Do you believe your Creator should be the most important?


### ~ Pass the Test ~
What are you confident will last forever? When you follow and have Faith in Jesus Christ, you know you will have eternal life with Him. Living a life that puts God at the top of what is important to you makes life worth living and helps you pass all of life's tests. It is never too late to put Him first.

# Chapter 45

## *The Future*

Do you ever wonder what the future holds for you?

I know throughout my life I have wished I knew what was ahead of me. I wanted to know how events were going to unfold so I could make the right choices.

When my kids were young, they must have asked what they were getting for presents at least twenty times as Christmas got close. They had, up to this point, very little patience to wait and see what the future would bring. I think we have all had these feelings.

Even as I have gotten older, I have wished time away so I could get to a future event such as a holiday, a weekend, the birth of my kids, or other events I perceived as important at the time.

What I have learned is that every day is precious and an opportunity for me to make the most of what God has given me. God gives us opportunities every day to make a difference in others' lives. That is what being a Christian is all about, and we can take advantage of it now and in the future because the future will continue to hold more opportunities for us.

Besides, we know the future. The most important part of our future is where we spend our eternal life. I know where I will be forever, and it is my job as a believer in Jesus to use what God has given me to help everyone I can join Him in Heaven.

### ~ Pass the Test ~
Live life for today, and help others in their journey with Jesus Christ. The future is eternal life with Jesus, and that is the only part of the future we should worry about because God is in charge of the rest.

# Chapter 46

## *Audience*

GOD BLESSED YOU, and you alone, with the influence you can have on those with whom you come in contact. Every day you have an audience. It may be one person, a dozen, or many. How does this audience leave each encounter they have with you? Is Jesus Christ interjected at any point of your encounters?

For me, I know that when I talk with others, if I make Jesus part of our conversation, I feel so much better about myself and those I am speaking with because I am doing it with Love. When I speak of how blessed I am, I truly mean it and am grateful. This was not always the case, but as my Faith has grown, I know God's with me, and I want to help others know He is with them.

With my work, I used to be afraid to offend my clients by mentioning God. If I offended them, I might lose them as a client which would cost me money. I was essentially putting money ahead of God. As my Faith has grown, I know God blesses me with clients, and He provides everything. Now I finish my e-mails with references to God. Because of this, I feel better and I know I am letting others know what is important to me.

I am not afraid to wear God on my sleeve and try to further His kingdom. When I involve God in my communication it warms my heart. When I write this book I feel a calming, loving feeling because I remember He loves me and He is always with me.

**~ Pass the Test ~**
Reach out to your audience and further God's kingdom. Let others know how much God's Love means to you and help others in their lifelong journey. I want everyone to know that I put God first, and by doing this I hope to be an encouragement.

# Chapter 47

## *Alone*

I AM NEVER alone. It took me a long time to realize this. I have had my share of down times when I felt alone and scared. I've been unhappy. This happened more when I was in high school, college and just after college. I was looking for answers and didn't know where to turn. Now as a parent, I want my kids to avoid going through this, if at all possible. I want them to know that when they are down or feel alone that this is never really the case because God is always with them.

My Faith was not very strong as a kid, and because of this, I made decisions based upon trying to fit in. When I did this, I justified my actions and sins and regretted them until I made it right with God.

What is funny is that most of these regrets that haunted me were small, petty comments or actions. I would do things to try to fit in or be noticed. I still make these mistakes from time to time, but most of the time I am able to pause and put God in the picture first and respond in a Christian way.

This is easier to do when I know God sees me and knows everything. I really don't want to let Him down. When I recognize that I have, I repent as quickly as possible.

### ~ Pass the Test ~

We all have times when we feel alone. This can lead to weak judgment, poor decisions, bad thoughts and sin. When I recognize my sin and ask God for forgiveness, I feel better no matter how long ago it happened. By giving my sin to God and repenting, I know God has forgiven me. I'm grateful for His ongoing grace.

# Chapter 48

## *Bad Things Happen*

WE WILL ALL eventually encounter death, unexpected results, heartache and despair. I've had bad things happen in my life. Some of them seemed so bad that I didn't know how I would move on with my life because I had no direction. At those times I was lost, upset, sad and very confused.

When I look back at those events, I realize how blessed I was for them to have happened. Through these, I learned what was important and how truly blessed I am. I can learn more during adversity than when everything is going my way. I can also discover how strong my Faith is in Jesus Christ. Do I turn to Him first, later or maybe not at all?

Here are few examples of what have happened to me. I understand this was not the end of the world, but at the time it seemed like I had no answers and my life to that point made no sense. I wasn't suicidal--just lost, worried and alone.

From the age of five, all I wanted to be was a professional golfer. I dreamed about it daily. I watched it, read about it, played and practiced as often as possible. I had a gift and was quite good. I won many awards and got a scholarship to college.

After college, I turned pro and dedicated all my time to golf. To do this, I had to save money, so I lived in places you shouldn't (bad neighborhoods that were cheap) in Orlando, Florida. I cut off all ties with almost all of the support people in my life.

I had a goal and it was to become a PGA Tour golfer. I played the mini tours and had some early success. I would spend 10 to 12 hours a day practicing and 6 to 8 hours a day working side jobs to help pay for my golf tournaments. I was sleeping fewer than 4 hours a night.

I was single-minded in my goal in life. After a few years of doing pretty well, I developed a problem. My nerves turned bad. I got what they call the yips. I couldn't stroke a putt without a nervous twitch. This caused me to lose all confidence, and I had to give up my dream of 20 years after dedicating my life to it. I was done with nowhere to turn.

I now had no money, and I lived in a slum area. I disliked the city and state I was in, my friends and family were distant, I had not developed any other skills, and worst of all I was severely lacking Faith.

Looking back, though, I'm grateful for so many blessings from that experience.

## Blessings
1. I learned how to have a good work ethic.
2. I know what it is to desire God in my life.
3. I know how important it is to have Jesus Christ in my life (because I was miserable without Him).
4. I made connections that have helped me throughout my life to this day.
5. I can teach golf.
6. I am a very good golfer.
7. I enjoy golf now.

8.   I learned from failure.
9.   I believe failure led me back to God and knowing that true joy comes from Him.
10.  Because I failed at my golf dream, my life took a different turn and I met my amazing wife and have a family that I love.
11.  I appreciate life and what I have.
12.  God gives us what we can handle, and I know now I couldn't have handled success on the PGA.

These are just a few of the blessings that I realize now looking back at my golf failure. God had a different dream for me, and it has been an awesome journey.

Death has also crossed my path many times. When I was a teenager, I had friends who died in a car accident. When I look at it now many years after, I can see the blessings God has given me. Please understand—I was only able to gain some perspective after considerable time had passed.

**Blessings**
1.   I appreciate life.
2.   I have memories that will be with me forever about my times with them. I am blessed to have known them.
3.   I learned from their mistakes (the accident was caused by their drinking) and will pass this wisdom on to my children.
4.   They are in Heaven.
5.   Even today, I make better decisions because of that horrible day.
6.   I remember the good things about them.
7.   I know God has a plan.
8.   I want to make the most of my life.
9.   I cherish moments more, especially with my

family, because of that event. I realize life can be short.

## ~ Pass the Test ~

Life will not go perfectly. It is up to us to live life to the fullest and realize how blessed we are. When you reflect, you can see that every bad event had outcomes that God gave you, taught you or blessed you with. Find your blessings and thank God for them. He loves you and is with you always. Only you can control how you view your life.

# Chapter 49

## *Luck*

SUBSTITUTE THE THOUGHT of being tested the next time you find a situation when you want to use the word luck.

I have felt lucky and unlucky at times. When I think of these times as a test from God, I react in a better way.

As a golfer, I used to want all the breaks to go my way. If the ball bounced the wrong way, I would get mad. If a putt lipped out, I would feel cheated and complain. What is funny is that golf is made up of many strange twists and turns which most of us credit to luck. Why would I expect everything to go perfectly? Who am I to think luck is with me or against me? Once I realized this, golf became fun again. I realized these are just small tests.

When I realized God is in charge, I had a different view of what was happening. These small tests shouldn't overshadow the fact I am blessed to be playing golf at that time, enjoying the green grass, fresh air and friendship of others. I now see the big picture and am more grateful.

Usually, the bigger the perceived luck, the bigger the test God is putting us through. When someone wins the lottery, the test from God is huge. There is a reason most lottery winners end up broke and their families in misery. They don't realize it wasn't luck but a test from God. When we know this, we make better decisions, starting with giving Him the credit.

We can enviously look at athletes and famous people as if they are lucky. Yet a lot of them have very troubled lives. When we realize it is a test from God, we know we shouldn't be jealous but pray for them instead to put Jesus Christ first. When/if they do, they will be good examples and have a positive influence on many lives.

### ~ Pass the Test ~
God does not use the word luck nor does He believe in it. When we realize this, we also know He can change things whenever He wants.

# Chapter 50

## *I Want*

MANY TIMES I have gone along with the crowd to hopefully gain from the situation.

I have laughed at inappropriate jokes, said bad things, been mean to others, disparaged God, taken short cuts, watched others do wrong, broken rules, turned my back on my beliefs and been a selfish person all to fit in or further my perceived standing with those around me.

I have been in sales a large part of my life. At times, early in my career, I sold products that benefited me more than my clients. Now, though, I believe the old adage, do what is right for the client and you will do what is right for you is true in all business.

Money and notoriety, along with stature, can make us do uncomfortable things. When I remember God knows everything I do, my decisions are easier.


### ~ Pass the Test ~

When you strive to glorify God, life and decisions become clear. And, when you do right by God, you will do right by everyone.

# Chapter 51

*Compassion and Help*

WHERE DO YOU believe the ability to be good to others comes from? Where do you think Love comes from? How about Hope or Faith? We use these words and have these thoughts and feelings. Deep down we know it is all from God. After all, He does all of these things for us every day.

Only the perfect one, Jesus Christ, was able to go about His life with Love and Grace for everyone. This is what we should strive to be like and do it without needing acknowledgement for doing what God asks us to do.

In golf, television makes a big deal out of it when a golfer calls a penalty on himself. This seems ridiculous because rules are in place to be followed. The implication is that most people in life will not follow rules if they can get away with it.

God gave us rules known as Commandments to follow, and often He is the only one (besides ourselves) who knows if we follow them. Unfortunately, we are quick to disregard His rules. We don't worry about Him, but only worry about ourselves.

### ~ Pass the Test ~
Pray to God to help you live life with Love and Grace. Pray for His guidance to be strong and to do what is right. Pray that you can treat others as He treats you.

Love, Grace, Hope and Faith are in our hearts and lives because of Our Father in Heaven.

Look to Him and pray to Him to help you live your life as He wants you to. He has given us all the tools we need and will guide us so we can offer His compassion and help to others.

# Chapter 52

## *God's Reasons*

HAVE YOU EVER been delayed or had things not go as planned?

When I travel in my car, I plan out my appointments to the minute. On occasion, I get delayed and fall behind my schedule. Sometimes I have found the route I was planning had trouble, and I was lucky to have missed the trouble.

This very thing happened recently. I drove through an area where a major accident was just being cleaned up. By my calculations, if I had not been previously delayed, I would have been at that location when the accident happened. I know God looked after me that day.

On another trip, my family and I went to the big, year-end swim meet for our kids. The night before the last day, the weather forecast changed, and it was evident we would not be able to drive home from Minnesota to Iowa if we stayed for the whole day. In the past, I would have been tempted to leave in order to beat the storm. This time, however, I took time to think about it.

It is amazing how much clearer my thinking was when I took time instead of reacting under pressure. This trip was about my kids and, even though I would miss work and it would cause problems, we did not hesitate to stay for the entire event.

The storm ended up being even worse than we expected, so we found a hotel with a waterpark nearby. Two other families in the same situation joined us. It ended up being a great time, and it will be a story we will remember.

The blizzard kept piling snow outside, but inside we watched the kids laugh and play all night long. What could have been a tense night for me is now a fond memory for all of us because I relinquished my initial desires to God and had a great night with my family and friends.

### ~ Pass the Test ~

God has reasons for everything that happens in our lives. When we believe this, we can have the right perspective on unexpected events, keep a good attitude, know God is in charge and actually enjoy surprises!

# Chapter 53

## *Pizza*

THERE ARE TIMES when I reflect on my reaction or lack of reaction and wish I had acted differently.

Recently, at Godfathers Pizza, a mistake was made with my order. It had been a very long day, and my family was hungry. I ordered the pizza so I could pick it up on the way home and meet my family when they arrived. I had timed it so that when I arrived at Godfathers Pizza it would be ready to go.

When I entered Godfathers, there was a man vehemently complaining about a perceived mistake. He was making quite a scene. I went to the counter, paid for my order and sat down and watched him—thinking he was being a jerk. They bent over backwards to make him happy and he left 20 minutes later.

I was still waiting and asked about my order that should have been done when I arrived. They realized they had missed it. Now I wasn't happy, and though I said nothing, I did make it known by my body language that I was not happy.

I had acted just like the guy who I thought was a jerk. I sat down and within a few seconds realized how I could have acted better. People make mistakes, and it was obvious this establishment was having a bad day. It didn't make anyone feel better or make the situation any better when I acted this way. I didn't treat others as more important than myself.

### ~ Pass the Test ~

We can have a tendency to overreact when something goes wrong. The more we react with Love and Grace, the better we will handle these situations. After all, God shows us Love and Grace daily for the sins we commit.

# Chapter 54

## *Why Am I So Blessed?*

AS MY FAITH grew, I became troubled by how blessed I was. For a long time I didn't understand why I was so blessed with material blessings, but now I have a better grasp of what God is doing.

My life's path took me from being very poor to having a beautiful, loving wife, two amazing kids and belonging to a country club in a nice community. I am richer monetarily than I could have ever expected.

We all have different things God has blessed us with. He wants us to use the blessings to further His kingdom. Like most people, I believe I have worked hard, but I am realistic enough to know God has given me what I have, and it is up to Him if I will continue to have these particular blessings. In my life, it is up to me to make the most of what God has blessed me with and to do it in His name.

Far beyond material goods though, no matter what happens in my life this side of Heaven, I know my greatest blessing is the Cross.

Playing golf is a luxury item that my family and I enjoy. It could probably be argued that it is not necessary and that money could be better spent helping others. I believe our Father in Heaven wants us to do things that make us happy.

There are ways to do things that make you happy and still further His kingdom. It starts with giving Him credit for the blessings you enjoy. Jesus Christ is not something you keep private. We must share Him with others.

Do those who know you know you put Jesus first in your life? They should, and if they don't you are probably not using God's gifts the way He intended.

What is important to remember is that happiness is a fleeting moment while joy comes from having Jesus in our heart. Always remember that Jesus died for our sins because God loves each of us so much. That is why participating in events that make us happy will have a place in our lives, but to have a joy filled life, we need to always seek out God and follow Him where He leads us. We need to serve others. If you only seek out happiness, you will never feel full but will find emptiness as you look for more in your life.

I don't know why I am so blessed but I do know God expects a lot from me and that I must keep putting Him first. It is my job to make the most of what God has given me and to help others in their journey with Jesus.

Believe that happiness will come and go but true joy, the joy that gives you goose bumps because you are loved so much by your Creator, will never leave. I seek that joy every day and also realize when I partake in events that make me happy, I need to give credit to God.

### ~ Pass the Test ~
We are all blessed beyond belief because Jesus died on the cross for our sins. This was done so that we may someday join Him in Heaven for eternity. When we have

perspective, we can serve God better. We need to pray for guidance to best use the blessings He has given us to serve Him.

# Chapter 55

## *Popularity*

As WE GROW up, it is common to wish we were popular. Judging by the shows on TV and the glamorization of actors, politicians and athletes, it is obvious that people watch them closely. Knowing what popular people say, do and wear is part of every media device. People try to mimic what popular people do. The only reason for this is because we, ourselves, wish to be popular.

What most people don't know is how truly hard it is to be popular. Really famous people have their every word and action critiqued every second of every day. They can't go anywhere without being hounded, and they cannot enjoy doing normal activities like going for groceries, walking in public, or grabbing an ice cream cone because they are being followed and reported on. They have to keep up their appearance at all times.

God gives us each skills and with them great responsibilities. How we handle success can be a great burden or blessing. When we use our gifts to further His kingdom we are doing right by God. When we feel our success is because of our own doing, we never find the joy of God's gifts.

**Pop quiz:**
Which life would you choose?
1.  Become a famous actor who has everything you could want but no concept of what it takes to spend your eternal life with God.

2. Someone who has all they need and gives all credit to God, wanting to use their gifts, talents and blessings to help others know Jesus.

We are all tested every day to make a difference in others' lives. We can choose to think of ourselves and do nothing or live a Faith-filled life and treat others with Love and Grace while giving credit to Jesus Christ for what we have and do.

God gives us the ability to influence other people's lives. His goal for us is to help others into the kingdom of Heaven. When we realize this, we have a better perspective of what God expects from us every day.

### ~ Pass the Test ~
Using what God has given us to help further God's kingdom will have an exponential effect on those we touch. Selfishness leads to a shallow and very uncertain eternal future as well as a lack of understanding of true joy on Earth.

# Chapter 56

## *Being Judged*

WE OFTEN HEAR the question "How do you want to be remembered by others?"

As a Christian this answer is relatively easy. We will be judged by those we have met by how we treated them and the influence we had on their lives. God will judge us by how we furthered His kingdom on a daily basis.

### ~ Pass the Test ~

Life is less complicated when we make decisions consistent with our beliefs. When we follow God's set of values, life is more enjoyable and peaceful. When we live life to help others know Jesus, we will know true joy and bring joy to others.

# Chapter 57

## *Not Got To — Get To*

Too many times I find myself saying I've got to do this thing or that thing. I usually don't mean it in a derogatory manner, but sometimes I do. It usually sounds as if I have to do something I don't want to do. I will say "got to" for things like cooking dinner, driving kids to practice, going out of town for work, cleaning clothes, going home, going to church, cleaning the house and the list goes on.

When I write down the list of "got to's" it hits me how blessed I am. God has given me so much. I now realize that most of these "got to's" would make many people feel overjoyed because having to do all these things would mean they had children, or food to cook, clothes to clean, or a career to pursue.

Perspective is everything, and too often I take for granted how truly blessed I am.

### ~ Pass the Test ~

Take time to write down what you feel is mundane and/or routine or something you classify as not fun. When you write the list, you'll get a different perspective.

We are all blessed in varied ways. Change your wording the next time you say "I've got to _ _ _ " and re-word it in your head. Turn it into "I get to" and see how your attitude and perspective change.

# Chapter 58

## *Smartest Coach Ever*

TODAY WAS A big day in the state of Iowa. My beloved Iowa Hawkeyes played their in-state rivals, the Iowa State Cyclones. The game causes angst for many in the state. This contest always results in one fan base being happy and the other severely depressed. Very few individuals seem to handle winning or losing the game well. What we forget is that it's only a game and provides brief happiness or sadness.

Many of us have the wrong view of competition. It is simply a distraction in our lives. These distractions bring diverse people together for a common goal for a short period of time.

Because we like our teams so much, we believe we have the answers for why our favorite team may have struggled or lost. I find myself questioning the play calling, the quarterback and the other things that don't go perfectly. When I step away and see how ridiculous it is that I think I know more than the coaches, especially coaches with great track records, I can get some perspective.

I tend to forget:
1. Coaches are more knowledgeable about the sport than me.
2. Coaches want to win more than the fans because they get paid to win yet they are the focal point of all criticism.

3. Everyone is trying his best.
4. Someone has to win and lose.
5. What is more important to know is that this game, and all other competitions like it, provide us with many tests and lessons.

Takeaways from a game like this:
1. We can all be brought together for a common purpose.
2. Our perspective between a game versus life.
3. Our self-centered perspective that we think we know more than others.
4. How we handle good and bad plays and winning and losing.
5. Entertainment versus God-centered activities.

When it is all said and done, how we react to the game, win or lose, is a very good indicator on whether we live Faith-based lives or whether we only live Faith-based lives when it is convenient.

### ~ Pass the Test ~

Always have perspective on what is truly important in life. Don't let entertainment get confused with your purpose and beliefs in God. Take time to interject Jesus Christ into these events (distractions) so you can react with Love and Grace.

Understand that these events last for a short time and we are never excused from acting like Christians, even for short times. God is watching.

# Chapter 59

## *Compartmentalize*

I AM NOT good at multitasking. When there are things to be done, it always works best for me if my full attention is put into the task at hand. As these writings were put together, I would often get sidetracked if there wasn't a set time to work on this activity. When I multitask, I cannot give my best effort toward any of the tasks.

Unfortunately, too often we compartmentalize our Christian values and beliefs. Do you attend Church and then minutes later turn your attention to other things, putting Christ and his people behind you? Do you leave Church only to get mad at the traffic or speak poorly about somebody?

Jesus Christ needs to be the foundation of everything we do. This foundation needs to be woven into every activity, thought and reaction we have on a daily basis. Too often we only give God short periods of time in our thoughts, and that doesn't help us nor does it further His kingdom.

Imagine if at a sporting event we reacted with Love and Grace. How would others see us? If we took a breath the next time work upsets us and realized how God wants us to respond, would our lives be better?

Is being unhappy and letting those around us know we're mad create a better situation for all involved? Would our circle of influence be better if we acted with

God as our foundation?

The more often we first turn to God for the proper response, the better we will feel day in and day out.

## ~ Pass the Test ~

Don't compartmentalize God. He should be integrated into every action, activity and response we have on a daily basis. We will never know God's full Love for us if we don't incorporate Him into everything we do. Turn to Him for the answers all day long.

# Chapter 60

### *Death*

RECENTLY, SOMEONE I respected died unexpectedly. He was 28 years old. I'd only known him for three years, but during that time he had an influence on my entire family. He was one of those guys that no one had a bad thing to say about because he was always kind, caring and loving. Our day was always better if we saw him, and our troubles for the day would be gone that short time we saw or spoke with him.

Many people want to know how and why he suddenly died. It is a natural reaction to question, to be sad and even mad. What we tend to forget is how blessed we were that God put him in our lives even for a short time.

I am so thankful to God for the opportunities my family and I had with him. Although there is a hole in our hearts, we are better off for having been blessed with his presence in our lives.

Are you a person who makes others' lives better every time you see them? I know people don't see me this way all the time, but this is what I am striving to do. Sometimes, though, I'm unhappy or act irrationally.

When I was younger, I was much worse, but as I have tried to live a Christ-centered life, I know I have significantly improved. Each test I encounter in life, I am getting better at turning to God for the answers. I want to be a person everyone says made his day better. This can only be done with a heart that is filled with God.

This means I need to do everything with Love and Grace. Imagine if all of us made an effort every day to respond with Love and Grace. How much fuller would our lives be?

### ~ Pass the Test ~
Turn to God for all the answers in your life and you will make a difference in other people's lives that will change their hearts. When you bring joy into another's life, even for only a short time, it will always make life better for you and for them.

# Chapter 61

### *Everything*

HOW YOU ACT has an effect on so many lives. Everything we have is given to us from God. We are stewards of everything in our lives. The material goods we have may make us feel good but they are only material goods. God gives us things to use for our good and the good of others.

Where we mess up is that we believe all these things are ours instead of belonging to God. He has simply given us these things as a test to see how we use them. Do we use them for the good of everyone, or are we selfish?

Because of the freedom we have in our country, we can earn possessions. We earn them by using the gifts, talents and blessings God gave us. When we use our possessions for the betterment of others, we are doing well by God. When we give Him credit verbally, we are doing well by God.

Yet, so often we forget He gave us everything we have. Our test is to first recognize who is in charge and where everything we have comes from. Secondly, we are to use what He gives us to help others in God's name.

### ~ Pass the Test ~
What we do and how we act can affect others. Do you put God first? What can go wrong when you put God first? What can go wrong when you put yourself first?

Choose to put God first because He loves you and will take care of you. Miracles happen when we are unselfish and do everything in God's name.

# Chapter 62

## *Adversity Is an Opportunity*

I ENJOY WATCHING college football. I especially like watching the bowl season. It is not uncommon in bowl games that a talented and once highly rated team ends up in a bowl game that is far below their lofty expectations. Almost always, this results in the team with less talent putting a whooping on the more talented but less motivated team.

Today December 28, 2012, Syracuse is playing West Virginia. Before the game started, the announcers explained how West Virginia was not enthusiastic to play in this game. At one point in the year West Virginia was a top-five team and they thought they would be headed for a top bowl.

The year went off the rails for the Mountaineers in the middle of the season and now they are playing a bowl game before January 1. Even though they have tons of talent, they had little desire to be in this bowl and it showed.

So often in life we face adversity and have a bad attitude about our opportunities. It was a blessing for West Virginia to get to play in a bowl. They have thousands of people spending money to root for them. They have abilities most of us only dream of, and they got to show them off on national TV. Yet today they came out with very little effort and missed an opportunity to use God's gifts.

Each day we have a chance to excel. We have an opportunity to do great things all in the name of God. We can make any moment something to be remembered while acknowledging who gave us these abilities.

### ~ Pass the Test ~

Don't let adversity bring you down. It happens to all of us. When we add perspective to the adversity and realize how blessed we are, we can make each moment great. God gives us the ability to have a great attitude.

# Chapter 63

### *Thank you*

IT IS ALWAYS nice to feel appreciated. When we make an effort to do good things for others, it feels great when it's noticed and acknowledged.

Throughout any given day many good things happen to us. Even on a Monday when we don't want to go back to work, it is a blessing to wake up in a warm bed, take a hot shower, drink a cup of coffee and eat a nice meal.

All the while things around us are happening like being able to watch our favorite TV show, laughing, listening to a bird chirp or many other things that simply fall into the unnoticed category. All of these things are blessings, and all of them are from God.

Like us, God wants to be appreciated and noticed. Take time during the day to say thank you. Don't just wait for big events, good or bad, but take notice of what He puts in your life every day.


**~ Pass the Test ~**
Appreciate all the blessings God puts in your life, every second of every day. The more you recognize Him, the better each day's moments will be.

# Chapter 64

## *Do You Try and Control Everything in Your Life?*

FAITH MEANS KNOWING God is in control and believing He has a reason for everything.

Too often I believe I can control what happens, but all I can really control are my actions. As I have gotten older I realize it is way better to let God drive me where He wants me to go.

I have people I love. I worry about them, yet I know I can't watch over them all the time. I can teach them, but deep down I know that I have to have Faith that they will be all right. I trust that God will watch over them. There will be bumps in the road, but I always know that if my kids have Christ at the foundation of their lives, they will be secure.

### ~ Pass the Test ~

Have Faith in God who loves you to lead you where you need to go. Odds are that most of the problems in our lives are a result of our own choices and times when we deviated from God. Remember, life is short. Eternity is forever.

# Chapter 65

*Serve*

WE NEED TO surrender to God and ask to be filled with the Holy Spirit every day. We need to give ourselves to God and serve others every day.

It is easy to go through the motions of life but not serve God in our hearts. It's easy to be too busy and feel like the days go by too quickly day after day. I believe we do this on purpose so we don't have to face Our Maker.

Even though I pray every night, I feel badly sometimes when I realize I didn't thank God for some great things that happened to me that day. Sometimes when I know I've sinned, I am embarrassed to talk with Him even though I know He knows exactly what happened. By keeping busy I give myself the excuse of not talking with God.

Every day we can serve God by humbling our hearts and in our actions. We can go out of our way to make someone else's day better. Opportunities to be nice and serve others arise several times every day. It can be as simple as wishing someone a blessed day, holding the door for someone or buying someone a cup of coffee. We also need to try harder and do what we can to serve others that need our help.

## ~ Pass the Test ~

God blessed us with gifts and talents to be used to help others in their walk with Jesus. Sometimes it is easy and sometimes hard, but we were given these gifts and talents to serve others in Jesus name. Don't let busyness be your excuse to be detached. Don't forget to give credit to Jesus. Life is about serving, so go out and serve.

# Chapter 66

## *Fail*

YESTERDAY I SPENT the day watching my kids participate in athletics. Like many parents around the country, I enjoy having the opportunity to watch them and am proud of how hard they work. Like most kids they enjoy some successes while they keep improving and have fun. As they have grown up, I've had them remember two things: Make God proud and try your best. We don't recite this as often as we used to, but we have it memorized.

As a parent, I want what is best for my kids and I want them to succeed. This year, my daughter has been competing with another girl for the last spot on a relay team. At this weekend's event the other girl beat my daughter with what I thought was a questionable relay start. This got to me, and I didn't react the way I knew I should. Instead of keeping quiet and seeing how this could help my daughter in the long run, I made a comment about the rules infraction to my wife in front of other people.

I believe I failed. I knew better and felt terrible about the comment the second I said it. I am pretty sure no one even thought twice about my remark, but I know I failed. I failed because I pushed God aside and did what I wanted to do. I thought it would make me feel better and justify my daughter's spot on the relay. Instead, I wished I hadn't said anything. I didn't make God proud or try my best.

Moments later, I injected God into my situation, and it became clear to me why I was wrong. In the past, I would not have turned to God and would have felt my reaction was fine, but now I know better and it will be a very good lesson for me in the future.

In the long run, this loss for my daughter will be the best thing to happen to her and to me because we will both be better for it. I have learned a lesson. My daughter knows she has to improve to achieve her goals, and I need to consult God before I react.

### ~ Pass the Test ~

When you take time to consult God about your situations, you will react in ways that make God proud. I don't like the feeling that I let God down, so I learned from this test because I failed. God always has the answer if you let Him help you. Take the time to let Him help you before you react.

# Chapter 67

## *Friend With Troubled Family*

MOST OF US know someone who has had trouble with their kids.

Unfortunately, drugs and alcohol are prevalent with younger kids, and they can do significant damage to families. Having talked with parents of kids with addictions, some of them have told me that it is easier to just concentrate on their kids who are doing well.

In one instance I remember telling a friend how influential our local church had been in my life. He was very happy for me but said it was too late to bring God into the picture for his child who was fighting drug addiction. This is how tough it can be for some parents.

It is never too late for anyone. Through Jesus Christ, anything is possible. History proves that one's life can be turned around by introducing God to them. Don't act like you have all the answers but, rather, recount how your own life has changed through Christ.

Do it in a loving way, and pray that the seed will grow. You may not see the final outcome of your interaction, but continue to be a good example, and use Love and Grace as God does for all of us sinners.

### ~ Pass the Test ~

Share God's love with others. When you do it in a loving way with no judgment, you have a chance to help others. God's love is not for us to keep secret. It is to be used to help others in their journey here on earth. Miracles happen when you turn to God.

# Chapter 68

## *Go to the Light*

WHEN YOU FEEL like an outsider and the world seems like it is against you, don't isolate yourself and stay in the dark. Walk into the light God provides, and take the light to others. Don't turn your back on God or be silent. Stand up with Faith at all times--especially when you're in dark places.

Currently, the United States is heading into darkness. Godless activities are being promoted and many of the Ten Commandments are being broken.

Leaders are putting government ahead of God and telling us how to live our lives. The times seem very dark.

One of the biggest tests we have in our lives is not to minimize our Faith. We are all supposed to do the most with what God has blessed us to help those with whom we come in contact in their journey with Jesus Christ.

When you have Faith you can overcome your fears. *When you have unwavering Faith in God you know you're secure no matter what.* Never give up on your Faith. Even if God doesn't come through for your situation the way you want, don't waver. What is the worst thing that can happen? Death?

Where do you go if you die and you believe in Jesus Christ? You spend life with God for eternity! Stand up to the bad around you with unconditional Faith. When you do, your fears go away.

### ~ Pass the Test ~

God loves you unconditionally. Love Him and have Faith in Him. You will be able to overcome all fears and conditions around you. By doing this, you will influence others in their journey with Jesus Christ. Do this daily.

# Chapter 69

## *Be a Great Example*

LIVE EVERYDAY AS an example you would be proud of. How do you want others to see you?

1.  As a good person?
2.  As a good friend?
3.  As a follower of Jesus Christ?

Which matters most to you? Is helping others with Love and helping them get closer with Jesus Christ the answer? Or do you want to fit in with those around you and not rock the boat?

When you don't rock the boat, people will think of you as a good person. When you do what others want you to do (even if you know it is wrong) you might be considered a good friend. When you live life with Love and Grace in Jesus Christ's name, you will be thought of highly and known as a follower of Jesus Christ.

When you follow Jesus Christ you'll make good decisions and won't follow others' bad choices just to be known as a good friend or as a good person. In your soul you will know you have done what God would want you to do.

Be a true follower of Jesus Christ. If others see you that way, you are probably living with Faith. Will you be comfortable when you come face-to-face with God? Are you proud of the example you have set for others right now, or do you go along with the world around you so as not to rock the boat? Make God proud and you will not fear God's judgment.

### ~ Pass the Test ~
Being thought of as a good person or a good friend does not automatically make you right with God. When you do everything in Christ's name, people will see you the way you and God want them to see you. Friendships and the way people see you will work itself out for the best when you put Jesus first.

# Chapter 70
## *Golf*

THROUGHOUT MY LIFE I have played golf. My goal has always been to score the best I possibly can. I have learned that trying harder isn't the answer.

Through trial and error, I have learned what patterns lead me to my best results. The two most influential pieces to successful scoring for me are concentration and relaxation. That may seem obvious or easy to do, but, having known hundreds of professional golfers, only a few have the capability to master both of these pieces.

Golf is a mental game. There are thousands and thousands of people who have the skills to be great golfers, but only a few have the mental makeup to succeed.

On the surface, concentration and relaxation would seem to be relatively easy to implement, yet they are extremely difficult to master. I have been blessed to set numerous course records throughout the country. I have shot amazing scores like nine under for nine holes and 11 under for 18 holes. Those days I was in the zone mentally. As much as I wish I could replicate that in-the-zone feeling, I've only ever been able to do it in short spurts.

You may find this hard to believe, but concentrating for 18 holes is nearly impossible for everyone. Even though a round of golf takes approximately four hours, you really only need to concentrate for a total of 15 to 20 minutes.

Why can't we master concentration for such a short time? A lot of it has to do with relaxation. When I am uncomfortable, self-conscious or nervous, I'm not as relaxed as I would like to be and then tend to rush the shot. I'm anxious to get it over so I can quit thinking about it.

Hundreds and hundreds of times I started golf rounds with course record possibilities. Then, because I knew I was doing well, I would become tense. The end result would be a mediocre round. Being able to focus, relax, and shut out any other thoughts of current scores or standings on each individual shot is extremely difficult.

I am now in my mid-to-late 40s, and my skill set is weakening. I can't hit it as far as I used to. I don't practice enough to save the bad shots which results in higher scores, yet my handicap has gotten better by two shots in the last couple of years. Why the improvement? Most of it is due to relaxation.

Why am I more relaxed?

1. I don't care as much as I used to.
2. I play the same courses, so I am comfortable with my surroundings.
3. I play with friends.
4. I understand how blessed I am and truly appreciate what God is letting me do at that time.

Every time I interject God, into the picture, I realize how blessed I am and I feel relaxed. Sure I still miss two-foot putts, but it is only because I let my own mind take over and tense up. When I put God first, I relax. When I concentrate on Him and what He does for me, I worry less and enjoy life more.

My golf story is no different than what happens to us in everyday life. Relaxation is often the key to success in many things we do. Being tense or worrying is never beneficial to being good at your job, being a supportive loved one, being a friend or enjoying life.

Recognizing what God means to you and feeling His Love for you will not only will relax you but make you a better person in everything you do.

### ~ Pass the Test ~
The more you turn to God and realize how much He loves you and has blessed you, the more relaxed you will be. The better outlook you have on life, the more successful you will be in all endeavors you encounter in a day, week, year and lifetime.

# Chapter 71

## *Smile When You Talk*

I HAVE BEEN a successful businessman for over 20 years now. I attribute it to two things: I care about my clients, and I smile when I talk with them.

Obviously to be really good at what you do, you need to care about your customers. The key to that is putting their needs ahead of your own needs. This is sometimes difficult, but it is paramount to long-term success.

The less obvious key is smiling when speaking. When you smile as you talk, you will have friendliness in your voice and a pleasant countenance that draws people in.

Have you ever noticed people who always seem to be in a good mood? I admire them because they don't seem to let life get them down. We can all replicate this by smiling as often as possible when we talk with others.

Oddly, I find it easier to smile when I talk with people I don't know well than with my close friends and loved ones. The reason I let my guard down with them is because I don't feel the need to impress them. In fact, they are my sounding board for complaining about perceived injustices. I've learned that I need to vent, but the better way to do it is to vent to God rather than bringing everyone around me into it.

When I let God fill my heart, it is easier to change my expression. Let the joy in your heart come out with smiles. It makes life more pleasant for everyone.

Unhappiness is a result of thinking about ourselves and the world around us and not realizing how much God loves us and not noticing or appreciating the blessings He has given us.

### ~ Pass the Test ~

It is easy to smile when you realize how much God loves you. Changing your attitude can start with a smile. When you speak with a smile, you can make everyone around you feel good. Thank you, God, for all my blessings.

# Chapter 72

*Proof*

HOW OFTEN DO you have events in which you praise God? It happens when we get married, our child is born, Christmas, and even when our favorite team wins. Yet when things don't go as we wish, we question God and wonder if He has changed.

Do we believe God should always make our lives perfect or easy? Should we not have to prove our unfailing Faith to our Creator?

He gives us numerous chances to prove our Faith. Every moment of every day we have the ability to prove our Faith. We do not lack for opportunities in which we can be Faithful in how we act with others or pray to God and follow His ways. Our Father in Heaven has already proven Himself to us. We are the ones that need to prove ourselves to Him.

Follow with 100% certainty that He is with us all the time. In the end we will be with Him throughout eternity.

### ~ Pass the Test ~
Faith is hard and is required every day. It is trusting in God at all times. He proved Himself to us through Jesus Christ's life and death. When we believe this, our sins are forgiven, life is filled with joy and earthly death equals eternal life with Him.

# Chapter 73

*Who Am I to Judge?*

WHO AM I to think I am good but others are bad? Only God knows what everyone does and what is in our hearts and souls.

Who am I to question what happens to me or to others? God is in charge and I am not to question Him but to follow in Faith all the time.

All any of us can do is follow with Faith and do everything in His name. We are not here to judge but to help everyone we can by using all our time, talents, and blessings to help them connect with God.

**~ Pass the Test ~**
God is in control. Who am I to judge or question? God loves each of us equally. He creates all our situations, and if we walk in Faith we have nothing to worry about because of the cross and the promise God made to us.

# Chapter 74

*Effort*

WHAT WOULD DO more good for those around you: gifts or God?

It is easy to give money or material goods to others, but if we really want to change someone's life, God is the everlasting answer. Money lasts for a short time: God changes lives forever. It takes effort to set your own life aside to help others' hearts, but often when something is easy it's short lasting.

When you have to sacrifice to put forth effort toward someone, it tends to have more meaning. Though there are no guarantees that the person will respond, your sacrifice has meaning.


**~ Pass the Test ~**
Life is not supposed to be easy. Work hard every day to make a difference in others' lives and their hearts and souls may be changed. Do as God always does for us, and live life with Love and Grace towards others.

# Chapter 75

## *So You Think You Had a Bad Day*

TWO DAYS AGO my brother and his family had packed for a visit to Chicago. His wife's best friend was about to lose her long battle with cancer, and they hoped to have a chance to see her one last time.

Early in the morning they were to leave, their youngest child woke up in pain. Walking was a struggle. They went to the doctor who told them they thought he may be having an adverse effect from the medication he was taking for strep throat. Their instructions were to be aware of the location of the nearest hospital when they got to Chicago. As a precaution the doctor took a blood test.

Later, as their family of six was pulling out of the driveway, they received a phone call from the doctor. He told them to stay in town because the tests had come back and revealed some serious problems.

The next morning after checking into the oncology wing of the Children's Hospital, they were informed that he had leukemia.

Less than an hour later they were notified that their friend had passed away. In less than an hour they had lost their close family friend to cancer, and their four-year-old son was diagnosed with leukemia.

What have you been unhappy about lately? Does it seem

petty compared to that one hour of crushing news my brother and his family experienced?

### ~ Pass the Test ~

Life is not fair, nor is it meant to be. When bad news arrives, whom do you turn to? Having Jesus Christ in your life gives you someone to lean on and someone who is able to take away your fear of death.

# Chapter 76

*Make God Proud*

HOW OFTEN DO you have projects that look so difficult you don't pursue them? How often do you avoid an activity or venture because the set standards seem unattainable?

When it comes to Christianity none of us can be perfect. This does not mean we shouldn't strive to be the best Christian we can be. If we swear and we know it is wrong but justify it because we do other things well, we must still repent. We don't get to choose which lines we can cross because we do other things well.

Everything we do has an effect on others. Kids learn from our actions. Others see what we do. We all learn from each other. Trying harder to be a good Christian does not work. We need to give our lives to Jesus Christ and put Him first in everything we do.

### ~ Pass the Test ~

We don't get to choose or justify which sins we can break just because we think they are insignificant or because we are good in other areas of our lives. Sin is sin, and the voice in our head knows when things are not right. When we sin, we must repent and change. Strive to be perfect, and when you do, you will have more joy in your life.

# Chapter 77

## *Day of Rest*

ONE TEST WE all fail with frequency is taking off one day a week to rest. We live in such a busy culture that it takes seven days to fit all our projects into the week. What example do we set for those around us when we don't have time to relax and reflect upon our own lives?

Our Creator knows a day of rest is important for us for many reasons. It is a time for us to rejuvenate and refresh our mind and body. It is also a time of reflection to consider our blessings and how God has worked in our lives the previous week. It is a time to look back on the week and see what we accomplished. It is a time when we can take stock in our shortcomings and how to improve. It is a time to spend in prayer with our God in Heaven and look for guidance for the week ahead. It is a time to review how well we use the blessings God gave us to help others in their walk with God.

None of us is perfect, and if we don't take time to review our week, we won't improve. In all the other activities we do, we usually reflect on how we performed. In sports we have a scoreboard and a coach to tell us how we did. In life, God is our scoreboard and our coach. How can we ever succeed in life if we don't look at the scoreboard or to our life coach to see if we accomplished what He wanted and how He wanted it done?

Our Father in Heaven wanted us to take a day of rest for

all these reasons.

Spend the day with Him and check your results. Check the scoreboard and see if you had a successful week. He wants to help you and commend you.

**~ Pass the Test ~**
God told us what to do because He knows what is best for us. The day of rest and reflection is important to rejuvenate and improve. Nothing is more important than what God asks us to do.

# Chapter 78

## *Family First*

IN GENERAL, MOST of us put our family first. As parents we do our best to show how much we love our kids. We love them unconditionally, and we try to teach them the difference between right and wrong. As our kids live their lives, we let them learn from their mistakes. We teach them things about life based upon experiences we had before them. Our hope is to help them and prevent the same pain we brought upon ourselves.

This is all natural and Our Father in Heaven does the same thing for us, but often, unfortunately we avoid Him. God allows us to make mistakes, but He always has Grace and Love for us when we turn to Him for forgiveness. He gave us the Bible to learn from others' mistakes. He gave us His only son, Jesus Christ, to teach us, yet we will always need His Love and Grace because we err every day.

Sometimes we forget that we are all brothers and sisters under Our Father in Heaven. Tracing our roots is much easier thanks to all the helpful websites, but if we take it all the way back to the beginning, we all come from the same people, Adam and Eve. We are all related. We are all God's children. Shouldn't we treat everyone with Love and Grace as God does for us?

### ~ Pass the Test ~

God loves us all equally. None of us is more important than any other person in God's eyes. Be the example you want your kids to have. Teach them the stories in the Bible because, even though the time frame is different, the mistakes we make are similar to those made thousands of years ago.

# Chapter 79

## *Not Alone*

PUT YOUR HAND out like you're going to hold your child's hand. Leave it there and look over. Do you see or feel anything? You know Jesus is holding your hand. He is with you every second of every day to listen to you, speak to you, guide and help you. You just have to let Him.

There were so many times in my life when I felt alone. It wasn't until I was in my 40s that I realized Jesus was always by my side and would never leave me. This is what Faith is all about. Knowing something is true when you can't see it or understand it.

I know that now, and I feel His presence so I put out my hand more and more. I'm at peace when I put my hand out and know Jesus is with me when things bother me. All I have to do is talk to Him and listen for the answers in my head.

You should never feel like you are alone. Reach out and take Jesus' hand. It is waiting for you.

### ~ Pass the Test ~
Faith means knowing you are not alone. The next time you feel alone, put out your hand and let Jesus grab it. He is with you, will guide you and give you peace if you let Him.

# Chapter 80

## *Signs from God*

GOD CREATED EVERYTHING. We each see, hear, smell, and touch what God has made. Often we go through life without remembering God's place in it. God made a covenant with Noah and all mankind with a rainbow, promising to never wipe out the entire Earth. Hopefully you are in a place in your life where you are able to see God's work around you and give Him credit.

Sometimes it is easy to forget, and we need reminders to bring our focus back to Our Creator. These may be in the form of a cross, rain, snow, a sunrise, sunset, birds chirping or a rainbow.

Open your eyes, ears, nose, brain and heart to take notice of the millions of things God has put in your life. Take in all of God's creation and realize how blessed you are. Take time right now to pause and take in everything around you. God loves you because He created you.


### ~ Pass the Test ~

Max Lucado wrote a book titled "*You are Special.*" It only takes about five minutes to read, but it can change your view of your life and help you notice that God is always with you.

# Chapter 81

## *You Are Blessed!*

OFTEN IN LIFE we feel like life is going against us. We may be in a bad mood or feel that our hard work isn't rewarded. Whatever the circumstances, we wonder why life isn't going our way in blissful happiness. What is more worrisome is we forget how blessed we are. Every one of us has been blessed with gifts and talents from God. We have all been blessed by God's creations around us. Most of all, we were blessed before we were ever born with Jesus Christ's birth, crucifixion, and resurrection for our sins.

Since each of us sins each day, Jesus' life and death is the greatest blessing we can ever imagine. No matter how much we feel that life has let us down, it cannot compare to what Jesus went through for us so we can be at peace with God.

Never lose sight of how blessed you are and how much God loves you.

### ~ Pass the Test ~
Every day you should give thought to what Jesus means to your life. As much as we should celebrate Christmas and Easter for different reasons, in actuality every day of our lives is Christmas and Easter.

# Chapter 82

*Patience*

WHEN OTHERS CAUSE a delay in our lives or we don't get what we expect, we may get upset, uptight or lose our patience. However, when we cause a delay or something goes wrong and it is our fault, we often come up with lots of excuses as to why we caused it.

We're sick, our kids needed immediate attention, we received bad news or had car trouble. We justify why we caused delays or why we cannot perform at 100% but often don't extend the same courtesy to others. We are hypocritical.

(And, yes, there are times when people try to intentionally offend us, but as a Christian we should show Grace and Love as God does for us and not be easily offended.)

When we are impatient with others, we are moving into an area for which we will never be qualified. We must leave that up to God.

**~ Pass the Test ~**
The next time you feel you have been wronged or lose your patience, remember that God is in charge. He has all the facts.

# Chapter 83

## *Every Moment*

EVERYTHING YOU DO in life is a time to learn or teach. When we interact with others, different responses with different people will create different reactions. We learn what works and what doesn't. When people observe our reactions they learn what we are about. Do we want to be seen as people willing to give credit to Jesus?

Too often we make decisions based on a moment to fit into a group when the only one we need to impress and give credit to is God. Whom are we trying to impress, God or God's children? What is amazing is when we give God all the credit, it positively affects and teaches those around us. How do you want to be seen?

A great way to teach others is to give credit to Our Creator. Through Jesus and our complete Faith in His life and death, we can have eternal life—an eternal life made up of perfection and joy for all of eternity.

### ~ Pass the Test ~
Learn and teach whenever you can. Don't try to impress the wrong idols. Everyone is watching, especially our Father in Heaven.

# Chapter 84

## *We Learn in Different Ways*

DURING BIBLE STUDY today, we talked about Genesis which is the beginning of everything. This always starts a spirited discussion that can be upsetting for some in our group. Because none of us can grasp God's power or time frame, we all have very different pictures and thoughts in our heads as to how God created us into existence.

We often get caught up in the minutia and forget the big picture. After having time to digest the group's response, I have come to four conclusions. We learn in different ways, we need each other, we all want the same thing for each other (Heaven) and God loves us.

### 1) We all learn in different ways

Whenever we're part of a discussion, we are trying to get others to see things from our point of view. The hard part is that no one will have the exact image in their heads as we have.

I am blessed to have two beautiful kids. They both are smart but learn differently. One child reads books and retains information through reading and doing the work on paper. My other child reads and comprehends information by images in his mind. The clearer the picture the more he remembers. When he watches TV he retains a lot. They also see the world differently. They are unique. Learning can be simple or complex for each of them depending on the topic.

## 2) We need each other

Not all forms of information are helpful to everyone because the picture we each have and the way we learn is unique. Because we are all unique, we need each other to understand and navigate life. Different discussions, points of view and illustrations help each of us expand our understanding and cement our walk with Christ.

When we are open-minded, we will learn from others and be helped in making sense of life on Earth. Through time, discussion and consideration, we learn more and our views become clearer and more solidified.

## 3) Heaven

Our eventual goal is to be in Heaven with God for Eternity. We want everyone we know to be with us. This is why we help each other by explaining and teaching our Faith-Based views. It is all with the one goal of Heaven for all of us.

## 4) God Loves Us

God loves us unconditionally. He will never turn His back on us. Discussions I have with my Bible study group is a way for me to strengthen my Christianity, have a better understanding of how I should live my life and how I can help others understand God's love for each of us.

## ~ Pass the Test ~

Keep learning. Keep an open mind, and remember that we all learn in different ways. God gives us everything that we need, and it is up to us to process and learn.

# Chapter 85

*Free*

MANY PEOPLE LOVE to shop. When we buy something for ourselves or for others it makes us feel good. The feeling usually doesn't last long, though, so we tend to repeat the process. A great way to lure us shoppers in is by having sales. When we feel we're getting a deal, it piques our interest and makes us feel even better about our purchase.

Another way to lure shoppers is offering limited quantities so we feel an urgency to purchase now and have something that others don't. Yet another way is to give rewards that accumulate, leading to something free later. All of these gimmicks make us feel like we got something that was special for less. We got a deal which makes us feel good.

We all want to feel good, and it's one of the reasons we shop for deals. It usually requires effort to take advantage of the perceived deals. We have to spend time searching for the deals. We may have to spend extensive time on the computer or walk completely around the mall to find them. Effort is involved in this quest to make us feel good. Most of this is designed with selfish intent.

What can be so much more powerful is providing services to someone for free. It can be kind words, opening the door for someone, paying for someone's lunch, helping someone move, or just going out of our way in a way someone didn't expect. God wants us to

Love everyone, and when we do we reap the rewards.

Done unselfishly, the rewards can be long lasting. They can have profound effects on many people. What we're doing is using gifts, talents and blessings God has given us to make others' lives better. When we do it we should give credit to God.

More and more as we do unselfish things, often we will make a difference in people's lives, starting with our own. We'll find that instead of searching for fleeting moments of happiness (like shopping), we will have everlasting joy and the rewards we experience will be life changing.

God gave us His Love for free. He loves us and wants us to do the most with what He gave us.

Make an effort to get involved and help others.

### ~ Pass the Test ~
God puts you in a position every day to make a difference in someone's life. Do it and give God the credit. When you do this, you're taking the opportunity to influence many hearts and minds.

# Chapter 86

## *Gambling (Risk Taking)*

THROUGHOUT LIFE, ALL of us gamble. We calculate how much better off we will be and take the risk. It can be asking someone to marry us, putting trust in someone, investing money, or placing money on a sporting event.

I have done all of these forms of gambling. I tried all of these things before I truly had God in my heart and while I still foolishly believed I was in control.

I have wagered money on things like blackjack while in Las Vegas. I believed that I was in control of the situation and would win because of my skills and systems. I even had some amazing success at times. In hindsight, it seems silly to me that I believed I was in control. God was and is in control. He decides what is best for me.

The Creator of the Heavens and the Earth makes decisions and they are in my best interest. I do not know a gambler alive who hasn't made a promise to God that he would change or quit if only he could win this bet. There were many times I lied to God and prayed for this kind of help to win. What often happens is that those who do win big usually forget their promise, lose sight of who is in control and end up destroying their lives.

I read a few years ago that over 60% of all large lottery winners end up in ruins. Their families become dysfunctional, and they lose everything. Why do you think this is? The majority of these people do not give God the credit nor do they do what God would want them to do with such a blessing. Of course, this can be said with any blessing, talent or gift God gives us. Once we acknowledge God gives us these things, it is up to us to make the most of them.

Give Him the credit and make a difference in other people's lives in His name. God always has your best interest at heart. Gambling (risk taking) by its definition means you do not have control so when you win, give Him the credit because He deserves it. When you lose at risk taking, know that He did it to help you. Winning may have turned out to be the worst thing that could have happened in your life.

### ~ Pass the Test ~
God is in control and, win or lose, He is with you. He loves you and wants the best for you. Trust Him to provide you with the best results. Losing at risk taking can often be so much better for your life than winning.

# Chapter 87

## *Set an Example*

RECENTLY, I HAD the great pleasure of meeting and listening to Aaron Thomas. He is the son of Ed Thomas, a well-known football coach from Aplington-Parkersburg, Iowa. Ed was a great coach, husband, father and leader who touched thousands of people's lives in a great way. He was first and foremost a Christian. He put his Christian values out for everyone to see and gave God credit for everything in his life. All in the name of God, he made a difference in people's lives so that they would go on to make differences in others' lives.

I highly recommend his book, "*The Sacred Acre*," to truly understand how God worked through Ed. He lived life for the glory of God. During one of the more notable years of his life, Ed displayed God's glory and had an everlasting effect that would be felt by many for years to come.

During this particular year, 2008, Parkersburg lost almost everything to an EF5 tornado. Ed and his family were instrumental in the rebuilding of the town. Months later, a former player with severe mental problems murdered Ed. The amazing part of the story is how his Christian values came through then and still do today with those he touched.

Aaron, his son, was on all media outlets throughout the country within hours of his death. In his press conference, he asked everyone to pray for and give support to the Boecker family whose son had killed Ed Thomas, Aaron's dad. Instead of being angry at them, he encouraged the community to show love to the Boecker family.

In Aaron's speech, he explained that this is what his dad would have done and how he had taught Aaron to act. He said that he had always been taught Christian values and that he needed to follow through on what he'd been taught and believed. He wanted to be a leader and not a hypocrite.

Even though losing his dad was the worst thing imaginable, like his dad would have wanted, he chose to consider God's ways more important than his own feelings.

### ~ Pass the Test ~

When you are tested, especially in a situation that seems unimaginable, you need to set an example and put God first. Just like Job, Aaron put his Faith in God. Remember God is always testing you, hopefully not in ways as heartbreaking as this, but He is at your side to see you through. Turn to Him and let Him guide you in all tests.

# Chapter 88

## *Help*

MY FAMILY AND I attend *Lutheran Church of Hope* in West Des Moines, Iowa. The place is filled with the Holy Spirit. I have heard from hundreds of people who feel God's love the second they walk in the door. It seems like every care in the world is better as soon as you take in a breath when you are on the grounds. This place changed my life and helped open my eyes and heart to God's presence in my life.

During the sermons we often hear "Hope stories" from members whose lives have changed by submitting to God for help. Adulterers, gamblers, people with drug addiction, illness and unhappiness have all been changed by turning their lives over to God. Many of these people needed more help in their journey with God so people prayed over them. Lives were changed with these prayers.

Praying is your direct line to God. He listens and helps. He is there for you if you let Him in. Letting others pray for you, whether it is friends or strangers matters. Miracles will happen but you have to open your heart and eyes to see them.

How big is your God? Is your God the one who created the Heavens and the Earth and knows each of us intimately, or have you compartmentalized Him in your life?

As I look back, there have been many times in my life that God intervened and protected me. I think everyone of us can probably look back and see that God protected us.

He has a purpose for my life, and He has one for you. Let Him help you in good times and bad. Don't try to do it yourself. Let Him help through your Church, other people praying for you and your own prayers.

### ~ Pass the Test ~

Don't go it alone. Let God help you. He loves you and wants to help you. Miracles happen through God. Open your eyes and heart, and you will begin to see His miracles.

# Chapter 89

## *Purpose*

I KNOW I am blessed. I have a beautiful, loving wife and two amazing kids. We live in a nice house and enjoy life with good friends.

I used to wish things were different. I wondered what would have happened if I had accomplished certain goals in my life — like making it in professional golf.

I remember that significant problems with that lifestyle were that I was achingly lonely, made terrible decisions and didn't take care of myself. Success at golf was not going to do anything but exacerbate the situation. Money was not going to solve the problems I had.

I hung out with other people, and together we didn't make good decisions. When I'd had enough, I came back to Iowa and was jobless for several months. I finally had a job interview for a job I really wanted and prayed I would get it. I did not get hired and became very disillusioned. As I prayed, God opened up a door for me that lead me to my current job which I have been doing for over 20 years. It has been very rewarding in many ways.

Early on in my new career, God introduced me to the most beautiful woman in my world. I see beauty in everything she does. Because God brought us together, it lead us to seek out a church that has had a great effect on both of our lives.

This is all a long way of saying that God had a plan for my life. Even though I worked hard to be someone different, God brought me to this point and I don't look back with any regrets.

You are where you are now, and everything you have done to this point has made you who you are today. Use your past to learn to put God first. Walk with Him. Don't wish away your past. Realize God has you here now for a reason. It is up to you to see your blessings and use them to go forward. Make a difference in others' lives through God.

### ~ Pass the Test ~
God has a purpose for you. It is up to you to move forward with Jesus, and you can make that decision right now. When you do, you will have no regrets about the past because God has led you to this time with Him.

# Chapter 90

## *Violin*

IT IS AMAZING how God has changed me. I find beauty now in the simple things in life. I take note of all the blessings around me more frequently. I get chills or goose bumps more often, and I'm more grateful.

One example of this is the violin. For most of my life, I was into hard rock. I listened to AC/DC, Scorpions, Black Sabbath and many other bands which made loud noise with very questionable lyrics. I made fun of people who listened to classical music.

One Christmas season, I went to a Mannheim Steamroller Christmas Concert, which in itself was a God thing because it was not my cup of tea. I bought a ticket and went alone. The music was beautiful, but the violin really pierced my heart. I thought it was the most wonderful sound I had ever heard played.

To this day it almost brings me to tears to hear it played. It always refocuses me to God's Love for me. It feels like God is playing it for me.


### ~ Pass the Test ~
Let God work in your life and find those things that God uses to touch your life. Let it refocus your thoughts with His Love.

# Chapter 91

## *Take Advantage*

ON ANY GIVEN day we have numerous opportunities to make someone's life around us better.

When we are self-centered, we rarely go out of our way to encourage someone with a gesture or good word. We can be nice to others, but how often do we go out of our way to do something extraordinary for another. When you do this, how do you feel?

When I do this I feel great. I don't do it to make sure God saw it because I know he sees everything. I do it because it can make a difference in another's life even if just for a moment. When you do it in God's name or tell them God loves them, it can have an everlasting effect.

The premise of the movie "Pay It Forward" was for everyone to do something nice for another and finish the good deed by telling the receiver to do something nice for someone else (pay it forward). This would be great if we could all get in the habit of doing something nice for others, but every time we did this we gave credit to God. By doing this we would be paying it forward only with a lot more meaning for everyone involved.

Don't be afraid to wear God on your sleeve (tell them it's a blessing from God) when you have a positive effect on someone's life.

### ~ Pass the Test ~

Go out of your way to encourage someone today, and then begin to increase that to every day. Whether they thank you or not, tell them God bless you, or thanks be to God, or praise God and you will have an even greater effect on both of your lives.

214

# Chapter 92

*Love*

WHEN YOU LOVE someone, you see past their quirks, habits, noises, opinions and verbiage that are irritating and keep showing them Love and affection. If our Love is weak, we will let these flaws bother us and eat away at our souls. Only when we unconditionally Love can we get past these things.

Unconditional Love comes only from God. He has this for each of us. He knows everything we do and every thought in our heads. We cannot hide our hearts and purpose behind anything, and still He Loves us.

Give everything over to God and Love those close to you unconditionally. It's not easy, but when we do it, our lives will be so much better.


**~ Pass the Test ~**
If God can Love us with all our flaws, sins, bad thoughts and selfishness, then we can Love others in the same way. In fact, He tells us to.

# Chapter 93

## *Daily*

ARE YOU LETTING life take you on a journey, or are you intentional about your life's direction?

When we let the world around us dictate our lives, we will not be able to be the Christians God wants us to be. The news and sorrow we are pelted with every day is based upon those who are lost in their Faith.

There are exceptions, but, for most, it is a spiritual black hole. This is why most of us segment our Christian life between going to Church or letting life beat us up. When the world around us is missing God's message and we allow temptations to affect us, we tend to keep our Christian Faith under wraps because the world around us tells us we have to.

We need to take charge of our path and put God first in everything we do. This should happen hourly and not just the hour on Sunday we attend Church. Let's spread our Faith to others and not keep it to ourselves.

When we start helping those around us with Love and Grace, we can start to change our surrounding environment. Life is about helping others, and the only way we can do it is by putting God first and outwardly giving Him credit for everything in our lives.

Take charge of the path your life is on. You can do it starting today. It begins by putting God first and having

Faith in Him.

### ~ Pass the Test ~

Don't let the world around you dictate your life. Be intentional and put God first. By doing this you will take charge of how you see the world and realize how blessed you are. You will enjoy life more and help those around you know the joy you feel.

# Chapter 94

## *Voice of Calm*

WHAT WOULD IT take for us to be the voice of calm for others? Too often in today's world, we see the mob rule. People get worked up about something and everyone piles on in anger. Compounding the issue, technology allows people to anonymously get people worked up without being held accountable.

As Christians we must remember that God knows everything we do, and He knows what is in our hearts. Hiding from others while inciting anger is not Christian. Joining a group and becoming disorderly is not Christian.

We can all get caught up with emotions, especially when in a group, so it takes courage, Love and Grace to be the voice of calm--the voice of reason and order. We can have an impact on situations when we do it as God does for us, with Love and Grace.

### ~ Pass the Test ~

When you put God first before you react, you will make better decisions, and it helps you to be the voice of calm.

# Chapter 95

## *Hardened Hearts*

WHICH MAKES YOU happier and more fulfilled? Doing things to make you happy or making others happy?

This may be one of the most important questions troubling our country and world today. With Christ, this answer is simple, but without Christ, this becomes more problematic. I would guess that if we were honest, we would say we put ourselves first and then worry about others. Does this truly make us happier? At times I'm sure it does, but most of the time, when we make someone else's life better, we are at our happiest knowing we are walking as Christ walked.

There will always be takers in this world. However, because others are takers doesn't mean we should take the easy way in our own lives and be takers as well. If we have the choice to be a giver or a taker we should choose being a giver every time.

Too often we justify why we shouldn't be a giver and block out the fact that God wants us to be givers. God will take care of our needs as we take care of others' needs. One of the ways He does us is by giving us true joy.

Something that is missing sometimes is that we don't give credit to Jesus Christ Our Savior and Lord when we help others. This has been suppressed by the world around us. To have the greatest impact on others, we must give credit to Christ Jesus. This is one of the ways God uses to change others' hearts and minds so they can go on to help others.

Government is not the answer, and, in fact, I think it is the problem. When they take from one group and give to another, there is no heart or Love or credit to God for the assistance. It encourages hardening of hearts because many people forget where everything in our lives comes from. This pushes us away from God and creates less willing givers. We need to change this, and it starts with each of us as individuals.

**~ Pass the Test ~**
Get rid of your selfish ways. Be a giver not a taker, and do it in the name of Our Father in Heaven.

# Chapter 96

## *Get Rid of the Word But*

WHEN IT COMES to Faith, too often I allow the world around me to dictate my thoughts and encourage my lack of Faith. The world is full of so much bad news and it can be overwhelming, so, instead of doing what God wants me to do, I say but this and but that.

"But" is used when I lack Faith in what God can do for me and through me. God created the Heavens and the Earth and knows how many hairs are on my head. He tells me over and over to have Faith in Him, yet I say but to what I know I should do.

When I was going through some self-reflection, I realized I was coasting through life. Being a Christian and a good person was not enough. I needed to be more intentional and get more involved in helping others and do it in the name of Jesus Christ Our Savior and Lord. I felt like there was not enough time in a day to do everything, but when I analyzed my days, I realized how much time I wasted.

I had excuses for all the time in my day, but, if I was truthful, I knew I could do so much more in my neighborhood, community and Church. For me, this meant I needed to analyze my time more honestly and spend more quality time on what I needed to do and free up wasted time so that I could help others. This is the reason for this book.

I have been procrastinating on writing it for a long time and realized that by reallocating time during my day, I could bring it closer to completion. By doing so, I hope to help out not only myself but others.

By making a small change in my schedule, I was able to complete this book many months ahead of when I was planning.

Now I'm making other changes to try and have more impact on other people's lives. By making incremental changes, I will eventually have structured my days and weeks to allow me to help others in a more impactful way.

### ~ Pass the Test ~

Don't let the little word but derail your day. But is quite simply a lack of Faith--a lack of Faith in what God can do for you and through you to make others' lives better. Make changes in your day-to-day routine and see what God will do.

# Chapter 97

## *Don't Stop*

WHAT IS HOLDING us back from making a positive difference in others' lives? Our strength comes from our Faith in Jesus Christ the Son of God. When we have this Faith in our hearts, which is provided by God, we can do anything. When we truly know we have God with us, we will fear nothing nor will we worry or back away from people.

We will move forward in God with our heads held high and continue to make a difference in people's lives.

To be our best, we must practice and continue to try to improve ourselves. God has given each of us our own skill set which we must make the effort to improve. When we improve the skill set, with God first in our lives, we will be the most effective we can be. Don't be afraid or stop when things get hard or others ask questions.

Always remember we are doing what God wants us to do, and He is always with us when we have Him in our hearts.

### ~ Pass the Test ~
Use what God has given you and give it your all in the name of Jesus Christ. Don't let lack of perfection stop you. We can all do great things. God is all we need, and we need to share Him with others.

# Chapter 98

## *Kids, Sports and Activities*

BEING A FORMER professional athlete, I know how wonderful athletics can be. When done correctly they can teach great life lessons: work ethic, learning how to win and lose, sportsmanship, passion, sense of community and team, and the will to be better. All can be great life lessons when used in context.

The truth is, though, kids' activities have become an excuse for many of us parents to avoid the things that encourage us in our Christian walk. Do you use your kids' activities to justify skipping Church some weekends or use it as an excuse for not having time to further your Christian calling during the week?

If we are honest, which activity will have a greater impact on our child's life, sports or deep Christian relationships? Remember life is short. Eternity is forever. Putting God first has an eternal impact. Our kids' athletics are fleeting moments. It is up to us to keep things in perspective.

Christian lessons and values are the foundation our children need instilled within them. If we gloss over them when they are young, our kids are more likely to look for thrills in places we don't want them to search as they get older. Deeper interpersonal relationships are a better deterrent against sex, alcohol and drugs.

There is zero justification for a child to miss Church for

a game. Zero justification to play and practice during all their free time. Zero justification for us not to teach our kids where Jesus Christ belongs in our lives. Zero justification for putting activities ahead of God.

It is difficult to miss out on the all-star teams and play in lesser leagues, but as a whole, our children need the foundation to live a solid Christ-filled life. We will be setting our kids up to have more fulfilled lives which will help them avoid a lot of the pitfalls of life. Most of all, when the trials of life happen, they will be better equipped to handle them.

### ~ Pass the Test ~
Pour into the solid foundation and put the time into it that it requires. It deserves more time than our kids' activities and will have a far more lasting effect. Fewer activities. More God.

# Chapter 99

## *Humbling Experience*

I KNOW I am blessed in so many ways. My family and I are what you would consider upper-middle-class, and we get to enjoy having more options than regular middle-class families across the country because we live in Iowa. Iowa is very affordable compared to other parts of the country. Every other week or so, we enjoy a nice meal out.

This week we were returning from a swim meet and wanted to have a nice meal, but we were tired. We decided to eat at a national chain that would not be considered a fancy place by many people. You can show up wearing anything including a baseball cap. We were less than excited to eat there and not very appreciative of the place. To make matters worse we had waited 20 minutes to get seated.

During our wait, it became obvious to me that some of the people around us were extremely excited because getting to eat there was a special occasion. This was a really nice place for them to enjoy. That made an impression on me, and I realized how blessed I was to get to eat there. My attitude turned around just like that, and I felt blessed not only to eat at that restaurant but to be with my family enjoying a meal we didn't have to prepare.

It ended up being one of the best meals we have enjoyed all year.

**~ Pass the Test ~**
Nothing is below us to experience. Jesus spent time with the poor, the sick and the unpopular, common people. Don't take for granted the blessings you get to enjoy.

# Chapter 100

## *Leader*

ARE YOU A leader or a follower?

In high school I was a follower. I wanted to be cool so I went along with what my group of friends wanted to do. I knew in my heart I was doing wrong, but since everyone else was doing it, in my mind it was okay that I did it. As time went on, I found that when I excelled the most, it was when I became a leader in the activities at which I excelled, such as golf.

Over the years, it helped me become an even better leader, but not initially. I would like to say I started to lead others down the right path, but I had molded my life to be cool so I continued my bad behavior.

Most of my sins probably won't seem that outrageous for a teenager, but as my Christ- filled life grew I remembered those sins more than any other. They are the sins that bothered me the most because I did them to impress other kids. I have asked God to forgive me for how I acted and how I treated others, how I broke rules, how I felt better than others, how I cared only about how I fit in and how I only cared about myself.

As a Christian, the small memories bothered me the most. I realized how I could have had a more positive effect on other people's lives. I wish I could go back and change how I lived and how I treated people, but I'm so grateful for God's forgiveness and inner restoration and peace.

**~ Pass the Test ~**
Be a leader in how you act and treat others. God is always watching and He knows what is in our hearts. Try to make Him proud.

# Chapter 101

## *Disconnect*

MY WIFE AND I recently went on a vacation to the Mediterranean. Because it's expensive to take electronics, I decided to leave everything at home including my phone, which was the hardest, because I don't go anywhere without it. We had no idea what happened in world news, world events or sports. We completely disconnected from television and sources that usually keep us updated on world events.

Guess what happened while I was gone? I was totally relaxed and enjoyed the vacation to the fullest. What I also found is that I spent more time appreciating what God has done for me. I noticed more beauty, more miracles, more God in everything around me. It was refreshing.

This is one of the reasons God wants us to take a day off to rest and clear our minds to spend time with Him.

It is hugely important because without it, it's nearly impossible to really appreciate Our Father in Heaven and the part He plays in our lives.

Remember, to truly know joy and live life as Our Creator wants us to, we must put God first. To put God first we must put aside distractions. Technology can be an enormous time waster and distraction.

## ~ Pass the Test ~

Life is short. Eternity is forever. Take a day off from technology and spend a day appreciating God. Take time to thank Him and listen to Him. If you want to live life with joy, put God first. To put God first, try disconnecting from the distractions at least one day a week.

# Chapter 102

## *Shield*

WHEN WE HAVE 100% Faith in Jesus Christ Our Savior and Lord and know through Jesus Christ that we are saved, we can live without fear.

When we put on the full armor of God we can have no fear.

We will be tested with things that seem unbearable, but when we have God as our shield we can be courageous.

He's with us always, and He is willing to help us pass every test.

When we put down our shield and try to do things on our own, the tests become unwinnable and more painful. It is impossible for us on our own. We need the armor of God. God always leads us to the only answers that make a difference in our lives and the lives of others.


### ~ Pass the Test ~
When we have God as our shield, we can make the right decisions and not fear the outcomes.

# Chapter 103

## *Pray*

DO YOU HAVE any relationships with friends or loved ones in which you don't talk to them at all? Do you ever go a day, week or month without talking to your spouse?

To have a loving, caring relationship, we need to communicate. The most important relationship we have is with God. Praying is our communication with Him.

No healthy relationship has zero communication. When we're truly talking with God, we can hear Him when we listen.

Don't just pray to God when you need Him, but talk to Him every day just like you do with the most important people in your life. Take time to acknowledge Him through prayer.

### ~ Pass the Test ~

Healthy relationships have great communication. The most important relationship we have is with our Creator and Father in Heaven. Pray to Him. Talk with Him. Listen to Him. Be still and let Him work in you. When you listen and pay attention, you will hear Him speak to you in many ways.

# Chapter 104

*Be Prepared*

TODAY IS MY son's birthday. He woke up early and was ready to go! Of course that meant he woke us up early, too, so he could open his presents. Since he was ready to go, my wife and his grandparents took him out to breakfast as I got ready for Church.

After showering, I was still moving a little slowly and not thinking clearly. I decided not to shave and just put on a decent, but wrinkled shirt and an old pair of shoes. Meeting my family later, we sat where my son wanted us to sit rather than in what I like to call the left-field bleachers where we generally sit. He chose what he has coined the perfect seats at the front of the bleachers.

To do this, he had everyone show up really early so we could grab those seats. They are great seats, but you end up seeing everyone as they walk by. This includes the church staff, who asked my wife and me to be the communion servers. (As we later came to learn, this is common practice when you sit in these seats.) Obviously, our answer was yes. God had called on us to serve.

This is an obvious example of God choosing me to serve that day. More often, God asks us to serve in more subtle ways. It can be as simple as wearing a cross necklace or giving God credit for your day. It can also be a dream He puts on your heart that you have no idea how to accomplish (like me writing this book). When you listen for God's word you will hear how He is calling you to serve. Break out of your comfort zone, and be prepared to serve.


### ~ Pass the Test ~

Be prepared to serve. God will call on you in blunt and subtle ways. When He does, step up and follow Him. Because He knows best, don't avoid it or stay in your comfort zone. It does become easier. He calls on us to help further His kingdom.

# Chapter 105

## *Blur*

MY DAUGHTER IS 13, and my son just turned 11. It all goes by so fast.

When they were born I had all these thoughts and dreams about what I would do with them and how I would teach them. Of course, only a fraction of my ideas went according to how I had imagined them. This seems to happen for almost everything.

It took me a long time to realize that God is in control and not me. Once I figured that out, I learned to relax. I knew the best thing I could teach my kids was how to have Jesus Christ as the foundation of their lives. When I realized I was not in control, it became liberating and I knew where I should turn when I needed direction and guidance.

### ~ Pass the Test ~
Life goes by so fast and we cannot control it. When we have Jesus as our foundation in life, things become easier. Follow Him and turn to Him and you can enjoy life with fewer fears and worries. Teach this to your kids and those around you because life does not go as planned, but Jesus Christ is always a constant.

# Chapter 106

*Participate*

I HAVE LEARNED over the last several years that listening to Christian music as often as possible makes me feel better. I am in a better mood when it plays in the background. It has an even greater effect when I sing along. When I do that, I become fully immersed in God. This happens in life a lot. Most information I take in during the day does not affect my thought process for very long.

I have found, for me, that when I participate, I become more engaged and the effects last longer. This especially happens when it comes to putting God at the forefront of my thoughts. I find that my thought process is better and clearer when I engage Him.

**~ Pass the Test ~**
Participate when it comes to God because it has a more lasting effect. The next time you're in a car, put on Christian music and sing along. You will be amazed how much better your day goes, and you'll find yourself humming it all day long. Try taking notes at your next sermon. You may find that the lesson to be learned that day stays with you.

# Chapter 107

*Revenge*

DOES REVENGE EVER make things better? Does revenge escalate a problem and make it worse? Do we think God wants us to exact revenge on people who have wronged us?

We know God does not want us to take up revenge. This means, when we follow through with revenge, that we knowingly run from God. We can also count on it turning out badly.

Thus, when we run away from God to do our own thing, the results are not good. This is true for all occasions. When we do what we know God would not want us to do, it will never turn out well.

### ~ Pass the Test ~
What difference could we make if we did what God wanted us to do? Follow His way, turn to Him in all circumstances and our lives and the lives of those with whom we come in contact, will be better. We will have to have a change of heart to be able to want to follow His way.

# Chapter 108

*Answers*

CURRENTLY, I HAVE heard of lots of turmoil happening to people I know or have heard of. It ranges from divorces to bankruptcies to dysfunction within the family dynamic. Because of these unpleasant happenings many people's lives are affected. The saddest part to me about these different cases is that most of these problems seem to be happening because they are trying to take control of their lives and are pulling away from God.

All of these situations are happening to people who are churchgoers but appear to be unaffected by God's truth when facing tough times.

We are taught to live a life based on living a deep and sincere life of Faith, not to just put God in a small slot of our weekly schedules.

From what I can tell, these people are struggling because they believe they have the answers, but there are no real solutions without applying Jesus Christ's principles.

**Can you name any situation for which God is not the answer?**

When we don't include God in the situation we find misery.

Most of us would rather turn away and continue

screwing up than turn and face God.

### ~ Pass the Test ~

Don't turn away from God when you screw up. He has all the answers. We may not like the answers, but He is always right. When we disregard Him, things will not turn out well. Turn to Him always.

# Chapter 109
## *I Understand*

MY FAMILY, MANY friends, thousands and thousands of Iowans and I are diehard Iowa Hawkeye fans. We have been very blessed to have had two great coaches over the last 35+ years. Over that time, we have made it to many bowl games and reached heights that should not be possible.

We have a huge disadvantage when it comes to recruiting players because of our state make up. Our coaches have to be exceptional to even get us to a bowl game because we usually have a recruiting class ranked 40th or below in the country. We are fortunate to have a few college-worthy talents per year.

For the last 16 years, Kirk Ferentz has been our coach. He has been unbelievably good. In back-to-back years, we finished seventh in the country. It's amazing when you compare the talent he has to powerhouse programs throughout the country. Recently, the Hawkeyes have struggled.

The last few years have been mediocre. In 2014, we had a rather easy schedule, and it looked promising. Expectations were high, but the season has been mediocre and some of our losses have been hard to watch. Fans, announcers, talk radio and even hardcore fans have begun to turn on Coach Ferentz.

People who have sung his praises for many years are

now asking for him to step down. I have even found myself seriously questioning the team and his coaching. Even though I know what he has done is remarkable, I have let my emotions and what I hear erode my confidence in a coach who has done a phenomenal job.

After the most recent humiliating loss, I couldn't stop my disgust with the team and I was boiling internally. The whole Hawkeye fan base had been voicing their opinion, and I was quietly agreeing with them. Then it hit me.

This is similar to the followers of Jesus Christ. Jesus had proven He was God through His works, words and actions. He had performed miracles that only God could perform, and His followers made it clear they believed in Him with all their hearts. Yet when the public opinion went against Him, his followers kept quiet, ran and even betrayed Him.

Now I am not saying Coach Ferentz is God, but I can see how I let my mind be swayed even when all the data and proof was there for me to analyze. Even when the facts stand, we can still make rash decisions based upon the emotion of the moment.

I read the Bible and wonder how Jesus' followers could lose Faith, but I do it more often than I realize and Coach Ferentz is an example of that for me.

### ~ Pass the Test ~
I understand how easy it is to lose Faith even when the facts and works completely disagree with my sudden change of heart.

Fact: Jesus Christ died for our sins so we can be in Heaven throughout eternity.

Fact: God loves us unconditionally and shows us Grace every day even though we don't deserve it.

Fact: God is in control.

Fact: When we put God first in our lives, we make our lives and everybody else's lives better.

Fact: When we lose Faith in Jesus Christ, we will suffer for it.

Don't ever waiver in Faith no matter the test. Life is short: eternity is forever.

# Chapter 110

*What Is Your Goal for Your Life?*

W‍HAT IS YOUR goal for your life? Really think about it because this question should be at the forefront of our minds for how we proceed from today until we pass away. For me, the end goal is to follow Jesus Christ my Savior and Lord to further God's Kingdom and help everyone I possibly can join me in Heaven.

The next logical question is, how do I achieve this? For me, I like to simplify everything because if I don't, everyday life will paralyze me with its complexities, and I end up doing nothing or repeating the same habits.

God made the rules simple: Love Him and everyone around me, always have Faith in Him, and always have Hope for everyone. He has given every one of us special gifts, talents and blessings which are to be used to help others get closer to God and eventually be in His kingdom in Heaven.

We are here on Earth to help others, and every day we are challenged as to whether we are passing each test with God in mind—basically, making our Father in Heaven proud because we have used what He has given us, to make others' lives better and in doing so making our own lives better. God always knows what is in our hearts and minds, so we must do everything with Love, Faith and Hope.

Throughout life we will make many mistakes because

none of us is perfect. And because God has a gracious heart, He forgives us when we own up to our mistakes and ask Him for forgiveness. His love for us is unconditional which means that it is never too late to ask for forgiveness, change our lives and start following His Word.

### ~ Pass the Test ~

Never forget the goal for our lives. God has blessed us with so much and we are to use these blessings to further His kingdom. Life on Earth is short, eternity in Heaven never ends.

# Chapter 111

*Routines*

WE ALL HAVE routines that we follow at different times of the day, whether it is how we get ready in the morning or how we react to certain news throughout the day. I'm sure you've heard or read the definition of insanity— doing the same thing over and over again and expecting a different result. Well, this applies to our daily routines.

By interjecting Jesus into my routines, I have been able to change some of them to bring more calm and joy to those aspects of my life. Since we all tend to have many routines (never ending circles) in our lives, don't think of the number of routines you need to change, just start with the first and move on. It will become easier and easier. Even though my intentions are good, I would guess that I've only changed a small percentage of my routines. I am striving to improve this percentage.

Eventually my new routine will be to interject Jesus Christ into all my thought processes.

Our routines and reactions happen in good and bad times. For instance, I drive a lot of miles every year and get frustrated nearly every day with just how selfish people can be on the road. Everyone seems to drive as if they are more important than everyone else. More importantly, we all seem to be in way too big a hurry.

My routine used to be to get frustrated, angry and probably raise my blood pressure. Now when bad driving happens around me, I try to take a deep breath and realize this is a test from God. I talk with Him and try to take in the beauty around me. I also remind myself that I am being judgmental about someone I have never met and that I have no idea of the circumstances in their life. They could just as easily be heading to the hospital for all I know.

After I go through this process, I become more relaxed, am able to let it go and not get angry and, in fact, feel better because I just spent time thinking about Our Father in Heaven.

### ~ Pass the Test ~
Try changing a routine you have by introducing God into it. You may find that you feel better and want to do it more often. Life will become more relaxing and restful when you leave everything to God.

# Chapter 112

*Be a Blessing*

LIFE IS SIMPLE: God is real, and He loves you very much. Heaven is real and its wonder is beyond our comprehension.

It is never too late to turn your life over to God.

Now the hard part.

Though every one of us has been blessed with gifts and talents from God, one of the biggest tests we are presented throughout our lives is to use our blessings to make other people's lives better and bring them closer to God.

The talents God gave us are to be used for good. Part of life is about discovering what we are good at and how we can best use them. We're all consistently being tested to prove our Love and Faith and Hope in Jesus Christ Our Savior and Lord. We also fail frequently, but if we repent and learn from our mistakes, we are doing well.

If we have Faith in Jesus Christ's life and death, we can handle any situation and know true joy.

One thing I have noticed in my life is that it is a lot easier to be unhappy rather then happy. Life throws so much at us that sometimes we let others know we're unhappy hoping that others will try to make us happy. Often unhappy people have found that being grumpy or disgusted is an effective way to manipulate others around them.

Also, quite frankly, being unhappy is easier, but it takes someone special and strong to not be crabby around others when they are having a lousy day.

This book is about understanding the tests and always putting God first. If you accomplish this with a pure heart, you will be in Heaven throughout eternity. The great thing about this is that you can help introduce everyone you come in contact with to the author of eternal life.


### ~ Pass the Test ~

When I first began writing this book, my main goal was to teach my wife and children to have Faith in Jesus Christ so that they would be with me in Heaven forever. It did not take long for me to understand that I am to do my best with everything God has blessed me to further His kingdom. I hope this book helps everyone find their way and remember that life's goal on Earth is to eventually end up in Heaven!

# Chapter 113

## *Tests*

I BELIEVE THAT we are all here on Earth to fully live and participate in life! Each one of us has a completely different series of tests that are unique to each of us. We can receive the same information but process it differently. We can all hear a simple message at the same time from the same source, but we often hear it differently from one another.

We are all God's children who have been given life here on Earth. He laid out the rules and sent His only son Jesus Christ to live among us as a servant and to be our example for how to live. God also gave us the Bible to help us through all circumstances with examples and words from God.

With all this in hand, God makes life simple for us to pass the test if we just do what he is asks us to do. Have Faith in God, Love God and those around you, and have Hope for all that they can pass the tests and be in Heaven with Him forever.

Now the hard part is that we are all given completely different circumstances and challenges to test our Faith and see how we respond and if we implement the three principles God gave us (Love, Faith, Hope). He knows we cannot pass every test, but He is so wonderful that He simply wants us to acknowledge our mistakes and ask for forgiveness. He also Loves us so much that He will let us change our lives at any time, whenever we are ready, to follow His three principles. The only catch is that we never know when our game will end.

Are we really willing to risk eternity in Heaven just so we can be tormented here on Earth? Our time on Earth amounts to less than one grain of sand on a never-ending beach of sand. What is the worst thing that can happen to us if we follow God's three principles? We will be happier and help make others' lives happier. Is it work? Of course it is. Any road we travel is work, but this one leads to eternal happiness.

I believe we are all given different information and circumstances to see how we respond. God knows what is in our hearts so we cannot fool Him. Our hearts must be pure and to help, He gave us the Bible, the Spirit and His church to use whenever we want. It is never too late to pass the tests God gives us.

Do yourself a favor and spend an hour and then a day noticing that everything in your life is a test. You will get a different perspective to everything that happens in your life and more clarity as to how to pass the tests. It is amazing what happens when you realize God is giving you information to see what your mind thinks and how your heart feels. There is never a time when you are not being tested. Even in the quiet times you can spend time with God by praying and talking with Him.

The first time I tried to apply the test theory, I was watching the news at night. This happened to be an overly bad night of news. There was an earthquake in Haiti that, to many of us, is disregarded because it is not in our backyard, but when we hear this we have a thought or response. It may be just a fleeting moment, but we think that event is terrible or we may have no reaction at all (both reactions are how we responded to the test).

Others may say a prayer, and others may use their gifts and talents to see how they can help. I do not know what God expects of you because that is between you and God, but He does know what is in our hearts and He does speak to us and put images in our heads. We all have a voice in our head many times a day, and I believe it is God telling us what is right and what we can do. A lot of times the voice we hear in our heads is our own thoughts, but I know if we ask God for help, we will pick out His answer.

### ~ Pass the Test ~

Everything that happens to you in life is a test. There is never a time when interjecting Jesus Christ Our Savior and Lord into the equation will not result in a better decision or thought process. The more you can recognize the tests around you and how to respond to them, the better and happier your life will be. You can never go wrong by putting Jesus first in thought or in action.

# Chapter 114

## *This Side of Heaven*

LIFE ON THIS side of Heaven is made up of tests. These tests are made to prove our Faith in Jesus Christ and His life and death. You see, when we have this Faith we know that Jesus died for our sins so that we can be in Heaven for eternity. God knows that we all sin every day. Those who ask for forgiveness, realizing their mistakes and learning from their mistakes, are passing the tests. Here's a sample of tests we may not recognize that happen during the day;

Do you give consideration to your attitude when you wake up?

Do you pray to God during the day?

What is your response to news that you hear (you can have a myriad of responses in your head)?

Does your mood towards others change throughout the day?

Do you gossip?

Do you go out of your way to help others?

Do you notice the beauty and blessings around you?

Are you thankful?

Do you praise God?

Do you treat everyone equally?

Is life about you or others?

Do you ask for forgiveness for your sins?

Do you lie during the day?

Do you think about how truly blessed you are through Jesus because you know you can be in Heaven for eternity even though you are a sinner?

These are just a few. If we think about it, we are being tested and the only way to pass the test is if our heart is pure with Love for God. God knows if our heart and actions are pure. We cannot fool Him. If we have been harmed or wronged it is not our job to judge, we can trust that God will when the time comes.

This lesson is one of the most important. When we judge others we are trying to take the place of God. This is not our job. We need to leave the judging to God. When we do, much of the unhappiness will be gone in our lives.

Most of us do not like tests, especially hard ones. Life is hard but the cool thing about these tests is that God will help us if we ask for His help. We can ask for help through our own prayers or from those in the Church. When we really pray for the answer, God will give it to us.

For me, I can see my answer and the one God gave me. It used to be hard to choose between them, but deep down

I always knew if I was doing right or wrong. I am very thankful that God has allowed me to live this long so that I could change my way of thinking and make it a habit to choose the right answer more often. It also allowed me the chance to ask forgiveness for all my mistakes. I am not perfect, but I am sure trying to be a better Christian and it is becoming easier and easier.

## ~ Pass the Test ~

Life becomes easier when we realize we are being tested and that God has all the answers for you. We have all taken tests. How did you feel when you aced a test? For me it is a great feeling to know that I've done well on a test. When we take life's tests with God in mind, we will feel great joy in knowing we are doing well by Him.

# Chapter 115

*Rules of Life*

GOD LOVES US so much because we are all His children. No one is better or worse than anyone else. To help us through life God gave us rules to follow, and if we do follow them, we will spend eternity with Him in Heaven. This is amazing. The rules are based on three principles:

Have Faith in Jesus Christ our Savior and Lord as the Son of God

Love God and everyone around you

Hope for everyone that through repentance and belief in Jesus Christ they can enter God's Kingdom

God had ten rules that he believed to be so important that he had them carved into stone. These are known as the Ten Commandments, and they are concrete rules with no gray area.

God knew we needed a Savior so he sent his only son, Jesus Christ, to earth to show us how to live our lives under the three principles of Love, Faith and Hope while abiding by the Ten Commandments. Jesus was our teacher because God knew we would sin. We all sin, but God is amazing because when we confess our sin, He forgives us. If we haven't confessed our sin, then we are missing the boat on Faith.

We are being tested every second of every day from

what we think to how we act in every circumstance. We will not get every test right and thus we sin, but we have the opportunity repent and make right our errors and not do them again. This is the reason for this book. I want everyone to be in Heaven with God for eternity and it starts with these three principles--Love, Faith and Hope. It is never too late to find your way, and God will forgive you because you are His child.

Here are a few of the tests and lessons that I have noticed and learned. Every day we either witness or participate in many events. When we interject Jesus Christ into our thought process, we will experience true joy like never before. We will not be afraid of life nor death. We will live with His inner peace and will strive to do what is right. We will try to make the lives around us happier and better.

The tests are very hard, but the answer is always the same. Jesus.

Your job on Earth is to get to know Jesus. Read the Bible and be with the Church. Learn and you'll be able to handle every test. If every one of us thought about Jesus when we had to react, we would be more apt to make great decisions. We will not always make the right decision, but most of the time it will be because we did not ask Jesus.

### ~ Pass the Test ~
God gave us the Ten Commandments to follow without pause. He told us to live our lives with Love, Faith, and Hope (with Love being the most important). To deviate from this is to go against God and what He has told us to do.

# Chapter 116

## *The Bible*

THE BIBLE IS God teaching us through His word with His own hand chosen examples. He gave us rules to follow that include the principles of Love, Faith and Hope, to put forward in our daily lives.

He made us each different from one another, and we can learn from each other and sometimes all together. We have been given our own set of tests that are unique to each of us. We are all put into different situations, and we all process information differently but the answer to the tests is always the same—Jesus!

The Bible is not to be taken out of context. This happens when individuals use one example like stoning individuals for wrong actions to believe this is how we should act presently or, conversely, dismissing the context of the whole book. The Bible in its entirety is meant to cement the three principles we should live by.

Every lesson in the Bible can be traced back to at least one, if not all three, of the principles God wants us to follow.

Many people relate to the New Testament because it is documented experiences Jesus went through and taught to those around Him. I believe God knew that as generations became farther removed from when Jesus walked the earth, humans would not believe the Bible unless there was proof. There is abundant, well-documented and well-chronicled proof of the time Jesus Christ Our Savior and Lord spent on Earth.

### ~ Pass the Test ~

The Bible teaches us the difference between right and wrong. It shows us what our reactions should be and that when we screw up we should turn to God. Remember it is never too late to confess and change your life. Also never forget that God knows all. He knows what is in your heart and soul. We cannot fool Him. That is probably the most important lesson to learn: God knows all. God is the final judge.

# Chapter 117

## *Life is Hard*

FOR THOSE WHOM much is given, much is expected. We all have varying degrees of gifts, talents and blessings. The hardest part about using these is learning to share them with everyone to help bring them closer to Christ, and to a lesser degree, improve their lives. This is everybody's calling. It doesn't matter if you are rich or poor monetarily, you can make a difference in many people's lives. The truth is, we are all rich because of the life and death of Jesus Christ Our Savior and Lord.

You, and you alone, make the decisions of your life. You can decide if you're going to have a great day or a bad day. You can decide if you will be in a great mood or bad mood. You can decide if you give credit to Jesus Christ for everything in your life. Think about the sacrifice He went through for you. This sacrifice is the greatest blessing any of us will ever have while on Earth because it guarantees us eternal life with God in Heaven forever.

Life is short. Eternity is forever. This blessing was given to each of us equally. We will all live in different circumstances, but every one of us has an equal opportunity to know God.

Do we find life to be too easy? Maybe we're not considering that we're being tested every second of every day. There is always something we can do to make a difference in someone's life, as well as our own. Spend time praying and seeking guidance from God and asking

Him to put on our hearts and in our minds what we can do to help bring other's lives closer to Him.

We each have different levels of material goods, and each level has different struggles and consequences. We are all required to use what we are given to encourage people to move closer to God by living sacrificially. In my many years of observing and talking to people, it seems to me that almost all people are jealous of other people and their financial and material goods.

The poor wish they were rich, and the rich either feel they do not have enough or wish for simpler times with fewer entanglements. When people have been blessed with a lot of money, they have a different requirement in God's eyes because He expects more from them financially. When we have a lot, it can make life easier, but there is also the potential to get entangled in a lot of material goods, traveling and the extras money allows us to have or do.

What can you do right now to help someone? What can you do right now to make a difference in your own life? What is God asking you to do to live more sacrificially? If you do not know, then pray and ask God. He wants to show you.

### ~ Pass the Test ~
We can all make a difference in someone's life right now. God gave us many gifts, talents and blessings to use to further His kingdom. If we are not using these, we are missing out on the excitement, satisfaction and joy God wants to have us experience.

# Chapter 118

## *The United States of America*

THE UNITED STATES of America was established by people of Faith. They did it because they did not want to be told how to live out their Faith or be ruled over by any other human being. They believed we are all equal and deserve to have an opportunity to live life and worship as we think is best. They wanted no one to tell them how to live their lives so they started a new country with God as the basis and freedom as the tool to allow us the best opportunity to achieve eternal life with God.

Government was established to provide basic rules which were based on the Bible to help prevent anyone stopping another from making their life better. Now our government has decided it will take the place of God instead. They force charity and decide who deserves more advantages. They do not treat everyone equally.

They're trying to force people farther away from God and trying to take His place. They make decisions on whether it is right or wrong if someone has more material goods than others. They tell you how awful you are for wanting the best for you, your family, and friends and want you to be more like other countries that have less. They believe they know the answers and should dictate them to you. They harp on a few bad things and overlook the many wonderful things about this country.

This is not their job. It is God's. He will be the final judge on whether each individual has been a good steward of what they've been given. If someone who is blessed with a lot does not use it for good, then God will judge them.

We are all tested in different ways in our Faith, Love and Hope in God. Our only concern is what kind of steward we are with what we have been given. If we're doing it to serve, we are probably making others' lives better and trying to bring them closer to God. This does not mean we can't enjoy life, but it does mean we should help others unselfishly. Government cannot tell us how charitable we must be. It will only be charity if it is from our hearts and not coerced. We will feel the joy of giving when it is our idea.

When I know I have done something nice, I get a tingling feeling that is awesome. You would think that would make me do it all the time, but I do not and am working on that. How do you feel when you make someone's life better? Do you get that feeling when the government rips money from your hands? If you are the recipient of someone's gifts, are you grateful? When the government gives it to you does it make you feel stronger or weaker?

I have had a full range of blessings throughout my life. I know what it is like to have little and need to accept from others, and I know what it is like to have much and be able to give. When I received, I was very grateful and strived to one day be the one who could give. When I finally had more to give, I was grateful and wanted to do more. Are you grateful?

Government was not designed to impose on our lives. It is only in place to make sure we are all safe and have rules God gave us to follow equally. God will decide who will be tested with different levels of financial status. It is our job to do the most with our God-given abilities and be good stewards with the rewards God gave us. Remember, everything we have comes from God. Our test is to use it in an unselfish manner. Government cannot be the judge of our stewardship--only God can.

We need to put God first again. We need to pray to Him regularly every day. We need our country to put Him first. Signs of God should be in our schools, courthouses and workplaces. We must not allow the few to take away our teaching symbols of who we are. We need a small government and a lot more of God. Remember, God is bigger than everything. He can do anything. He, and only He, can judge our lives on Earth and decide our final destination for eternity.

## ~ Pass the Test ~

The United States of America was established so humans would not rule over other humans and tell them how to worship. Government is not God. Government should not judge. Government's role is to provide equal opportunities for everyone while abiding by the basic principles God put forth for us in the Ten Commandments. These Ten Commandments are not to be altered in any way. Government needs to stop playing God.

# Chapter 119

## *Slow Down*

GOD GAVE US a seven-day week. Of that, one day is meant for reflection and relaxation with God. We all need to recharge our batteries and spend some alone time with God. He knew life would be difficult for us, so He wanted us to take a day and consider our lives and His hand in it. How often do you reflect on your week and take notice of how God worked? How often do you reflect on ways to improve and correct mistakes you have made? God rested on the seventh day after He worked which means we will be better off if we do, too.

So many of us only spend time with God when we are with the Church. As soon as the services are over, we may tune Him out and run off to whatever activity we have planned. This can be especially true with children's activities, or we may just be trying to pack too much into a week. Stop and consider: How satisfying are our lives if we do not spend time with God?

Can we really get the most out of life when we shut out the one who gave us life? Are our priorities messed up when we're not following His plan for our lives? Do we believe God knows best? He wants us to rest. Slow down in order to have the energy and guidance from Him to have the greatest impact on Earth possible. Can we pass the tests He gives if we do not take the time to see how He's working and also let Him help us fix our mistakes?

There is a saying that practice does not make perfect,

only perfect practice makes perfect. We can do better in our lives if we take time to see the mistakes we have made. If we're not setting aside time for God, we are guaranteed to be making more mistakes and not correcting the previous mistakes. This means trouble in our lives. No activity is more important than spending time with God who is the final judge as to our eternal life.

If Jesus came to earth today and came to your house, would you try to get your house in order? Would it be easier if you had spent a little time with God each week to correct your errors?

More God. Less me.

## ~ Pass the Test ~

God knows best. Taking a day of rest is for our betterment. Take a day off and spend time with Him. It is for your welfare and for you to set an example to everyone around you. More God time is always good.

# Chapter 120

## *Fear of God*

SOME PAST GENERATIONS used to live life with the fear of God. Now many in our government have disallowed God in our world. We, the people, have allowed the few to dictate that God is not allowed in schools or government buildings because of the separation of Church and state. The problem is that the separation of Church and state has always been misunderstood and no one has stood up to tell the truth of its meaning.

Our founders made it simple for all Americans to worship God in their own way and without the government having the right to interfere. Yet one judge made a foolish ruling years ago, and now we have a new meaning that states government and Churches must not co-mingle. If our founding fathers were here today, they would laugh at how something they made so simple was allowed to be changed so dramatically.

The fear of God, or the reverent awe of God, is the way we should all live. This means we should consider "how would God view this?" before we do anything. Imagine if everyone would give thought to their actions by praying for direction to make the correct decisions. We would still make mistakes, and we would still make self-centered decisions because we are human, but if we asked God for direction as often as we could, would we make better decisions more often? This would become easier over time if we practiced consistently. I think our society would be incredibly benefitted by this.

### ~ Pass the Test ~

When we live life with the fear of God, we'll make better decisions. The world around us benefits when we make decisions based on the fear of God. Being in awe of God makes us desire to do better.

# Chapter 121

## *Attitude*

EACH DAY YOU will have an effect on those with whom you come in contact, whether in person or through other forms of communication. Your attitude could have an impact on their day. Take the time to ask God what words each person needs to hear as you communicate with them. If someone is overwhelmed with life's concerns, you may very well encourage them by your attitude.

How do you treat your family in the morning? If you greeted them with a huge smile and a said "God has given us another wonderful day. Let's enjoy it and try to bring joy to others' lives!" what do you think that would do for setting the tone for the day? If you're like me, you may start the day off unengaged or prickly. The great thing about God is that we can make a conscious decision at any time to connect and integrate Him into the picture.

I have always admired people who seem to consistently have a good attitude. I look forward to being around them and think highly of them. The problem is that it is easier to have a bad attitude than a good one. You have to make an effort to look at things through God's eyes. You have to be vigilant so that the things that hit you over the head on a daily basis don't bring you down.

I know there are times when we don't want to have a Godly attitude, but that is a decision we have made and when we do, we are not passing the test God has given us. When we want to be grumpy, just think of the sacrifice Jesus went through for us so that someday we can join Him in Heaven. He took every one of our sins with Him to the grave. Because of this, we can live with free hearts, and we have the ability to choose not to sin with selfish attitudes.

Just like anything else, we have to start somewhere when it comes to our attitudes, so make an effort to be happy and share the joy with those around you. Start it now and when life gets going fast, slow down and bring yourself back to God. Try to control your attitude, and it will become easier every time you do it.


### ~ Pass the Test ~

We, and we alone, are in control of our moods and attitudes. Being in a great mood and having a good attitude not only helps us but also those around us. It can be hard work to consider our attitudes and how they affect others, but it will bring us joy and be a solid example for our spouses, children and other people close to us.

# Chapter 122
*Make a Difference*

GOD GAVE EACH of us specific talents, gifts and blessings to use while we are here on Earth. We are to use them to bring those we come in contact with closer to God. We are to use them for good and to help others. We will also get pleasure out of the results of putting these to use because we are living out God's desires for us.

We are all asked to tithe. This is simply a test that God gives us to prove that we know none of what we have is ours, but that it was all given to us by God. The harder part is determining how we use the money we earned to encourage and support others' lives. We are not passing the test if we hoard what we possess and only use it for our own happiness.

Another part of the test is to use whatever podium we are given, due to our talents, to give credit to God. We see some athletes give God credit when interviewed, and this is what all of us should do when we have the opportunity. When someone congratulates us for an achievement, we have our podium. How do we respond?

I have been blessed to be able to play golf well. I have won many different awards throughout the years. In my younger years, I always gave myself the credit because I worked hard or because I was superior. This was wrong. God gave me the talents and the podium, and He simply wants me to acknowledge Him on that podium. When we do this, we are passing the test and may have an influence on those who hear us give credit to Our Almighty God.

Over the last two years, I have had an opportunity to play with quite a few high school and college kids who are very talented golfers. Almost every one of them acted like Tiger Woods. They all had outbursts and slammed clubs into the ground. They all seemed to want to emulate him. They are not good sports at all nor are they fun to be around. This is what they learned from him when he had the podium.

Imagine if Tiger acted like Jack Nicklaus, whom I believe is one of the greatest sportsmen ever to play any sport. When Jack competed, he would put his past behind him meaning he wouldn't get mad and throw a temper tantrum. When he finished competing, he would graciously smile and congratulate anyone who beat him and tell them he gave it all he had and they were simply better than him in that tournament. He wouldn't blame bad breaks (which if you play golf you believe you are always unlucky) for his defeat. The one thing he did not do was give credit to God so we don't know where his Faith was. But, heck, it took me 35 years to find my way to God in this way!

### ~ Pass the Test ~
People are always watching us. God gives us a podium, whether it is in front of one person or before thousands. Be the example He wants you to be. Give Him credit because everything comes from Him.

# Chapter 123
## *Your Responsibility*

IF YOU ARE a Christian, then you have a fundamental responsibility to look out for the well being of other people. I write this because, instead of people watching out for one another, I believe we have allowed our government to inject itself into our lives in very obtrusive ways because they believe they need to rule over us. This is not true. The only thing missing in our wayward ways is our lack of Faith and belief in Jesus Christ.

As believers, we know that it is our responsibility to take care of the people around us and not something to be mandated by government. What we need to do is help bring people closer to God by using the gifts, talents and blessings God has given us.

I have some real concerns about things going on in our country. I believe the government continues to figure out ways to take from us, personally, what God has given us. I see others knowingly profiting while polluting the water and still others profiting while producing and promoting brutal and sensual television shows and movies. Added to that list are human trafficking, drug trafficking and abortion. The list goes on of unfettered, unbridled greed, sensuality, brutality and selfishness.

I believe we have choices to make of what we purchase, watch and promote through participation or quiet acquiescence. The more we participate, the more calloused and blind and stubborn our hearts get, individually and as a nation. We can't just turn and look the other way when we know someone is being wronged or hurt.

Fellow Christians, it is time to make your views heard. Don't let the few run our lives. It is time for all of us to make our beliefs and values known in a loving way. It is not always easy, but it is important that we all do it and as we do it as individuals it will soon be done as a group. There is no gray area when it comes to the treatment of other human beings.

There is no gray area when it comes to treating others how we want to be treated. There is no gray area in allowing teachings by television, schools or government that is anti-God. We must live and speak Christ-like values. If we don't, we're allowing other views more sway than they should have. We need to encourage people to want to be closer to God by revealing His heart through our lives. It isn't easy, but it is right. Be a good example in Love.

### ~ Pass the Test ~
It is our individual responsibility to spread God's love and ways to everyone. If every Christian lived this out, our country and the world would be impacted in a glorious way. We cannot sit on the sidelines and allow those with no Faith to run our children, businesses and country. God gives us many gifts, talents and blessings to use to further His kingdom. Make a difference.

# Chapter 124

*Separation of Church and State*

THE MAIN REASON for the search for and the founding of the United States of America was so that its citizens could worship God freely. The founding fathers made it clear that we have a culture based on Faith in God through Jesus Christ. Look at a dollar bill in your pocket and you will see In God We Trust. In many of their writings, they said you cannot have morals without Faith. In no document that they wrote, was there any verbiage declaring the separation of Church and state.

This is a recent phenomenon over the last 60 or so years when we had some Supreme Court justices take Thomas Jefferson's writings out of context. (This is similar to how people take a few words out of the Bible and use them without understanding the full context. We must understand everything in the Bible within the context of the Bible.)

The founding fathers wanted the Bible to be in every classroom and its virtues and morals to be taught to all of its citizens. The separation of Church and state was simply meant to keep government out of the picture and not allow officials to dictate what and how religion was to be taught. All were free to choose their own religion.

We now live in a country that has become corrupt. It seems that some leaders have forgotten that God is always watching no matter where they are and what they're doing. He knows our minds and hearts. The founding fathers and previous great Presidents warned this could happen if we removed the principles of the teachings of God. It has always been up to as individuals, parents and Americans to teach these principles, but when our government interferes in our schools, courts and businesses, then we need to be more vigilant and step it up ourselves.

It's easy to put this on our churches, but it really begins at home. Go back to the writings of the founding fathers and teach the youth of America what they wrote and stood for. Teach why this great country was established and never be afraid to talk about God and his son Jesus Christ Our Savior and Lord.

Our whole culture needs to change to the way the country was intended to move forward. It is no surprise that after the Supreme Court took our founding fathers out of context that many of America's problems escalated to unprecedented heights. Murders, major crimes, teen pregnancies, drug use, abortion and many other problems all increased exponentially.

Miracles happen when God is involved. When people have Faith, they do what is right. Get involved and teach the Bible and its truths. If we all begin to do this as our founding fathers wanted, we will turn around a lot of the problems that are present in our society.

As past great leaders of our country have stated, we get the government we deserve. When we stop voting and stop teaching God's principles, when we allow radicals to dictate to us, allow government to determine our rights as humans, disregard Godly morals, become apathetic to what goes on around us, and stop having Faith in God, then we will get the government we deserve. We get elected leaders who believe they are above the law in how they lead, and we get a corrupt and dark and scary country.

Remember, charity comes from within and cannot be forced upon us. When we follow Jesus Christ, we will look out for those around us. Use the gifts, talents and blessings God gave to bring those around you closer to God. Remember, God's Love for us is unconditional. It is never too late for us or anyone we know. That is what is so great about Our Father in Heaven. He's waiting for us to join His team and will never give up on us. Don't wait or procrastinate.

### ~ Pass the Test ~
Live a life of Faith and share it with everyone. Don't let government or others persuade us to keep quiet or not do good things for others. Everything starts with each of us, individually.

# Chapter 125

## *Which Side Would You Choose?*

IF THE UNITED States of America were split into two countries with two different governments at the Mississippi River and you had a choice to live on the East or West side, which would you choose? What would be your number one factor? What other factors would be important to you?

What would it be like if the east stayed like it is now, but the west of the Mississippi was governed by Christian values with no gray areas, followed the Ten Commandments, Faith came first for everyone and we talked and lived freely. Everyone would be treated equitably. Selflessness would take the place of selfishness. Which side, east or west, would you choose?

Think about that when you have an opportunity to vote for your leaders and representatives. Never miss the opportunity to vote, and always vote for upright morals. Voting for the right candidate takes work on your part in order to know the issues and what they believe. You will not agree on everything they say, and be careful not to vote for those candidates that pit American against American. We are all in this together and need each other to succeed.

Hold your representatives to the standards required by God. Are they using the gifts, talents and blessings God gave them to bring everyone closer to God? They must recognize that God gave them these gifts in words as well as through actions. As Christians, this is how we pass this test.

### ~ Pass the Test ~

If you had a choice, would you choose a Christ-based country or the one we live in today? We must take part in our political system and do our best to choose Christians leaders. If those choices are not available, then we must become more involved to make it happen. If we sit quietly, we will lose our freedom to those corrupted by power.

# Chapter 126

## *Hypocrites*

THIS IS PROBABLY one of the most sinister of tests we have to try to pass on a daily basis. Since all of us sin, we are all hypocrites. It is a reminder that we do not have the right to judge anyone and must leave it up to God. I am writing this book in a fashion which probably injects too many of my opinions, but I also believe God is helping me.

The premise to each chapter still comes back to God and His Word. The principles are correct, and my belief in God is unwavering. The book is made up of examples from my life that have taught and influenced me. I pray that I am deciphering these examples correctly to help you as they have helped me.

It is easy in life to discount everyone because you believe that everyone is a hypocrite. Though people waver and hop from idea to idea, God's word never changes. I'm trying to base everything in this book on God. I want everyone to realize how short life on Earth will be and how long eternity truly is. Life with God is not only phenomenal while on Earth but is exceptional for all of eternity.

It is your choice as to whether or not you have eternal happiness. It can begin today for you if you choose. This book is not perfect, but the message of God remains constant. You can make your life more satisfying from this moment on, but you have to follow your Creator.

You need to start noticing the tests you are given every day. You will discover that God is bigger than any problem you have, and He will be with you forever. You can follow His rules and principles. He has given you everything you need to be satisfied now and forever, but you have to believe and repent.

My hope is that, with God's help, this book will help you through the day-to-day tests and bring you closer to God. I selfishly want my family and friends to have this knowledge of God so that we can be together forever in Heaven. I also pray that it will help everyone because I know each has the opportunity to be happy forever if we choose.

### ~ Pass the Test ~

I hope that after reading this book, you will begin to recognize the tests around you and that the words Pass The Test will trigger an image of God. Once it starts, it will happen more and more often, and you will begin making better decisions in your daily life. If that happens, then this book was a success even if it was written by a hypocrite.

# Chapter 127

## *Zach Johnson*

IF YOU ARE a golf fan, you may know Zach Johnson. He is a former winner of the Masters and 2015 British Open champion along with having won many tournaments on the PGA Tour. After winning these tournaments, he outwardly gives credit for his success to Jesus Christ Our Savior and Lord.

In fact when he won the Masters, it happened to land on Easter and it was the first thing he referenced in his victory speech on TV. He gave all credit to Jesus Christ in the first few moments of his speech. He used his pulpit on a national stage to talk about his Christian beliefs. He is not the first athlete to do this, and he won't be the last. It was very refreshing and sincere, and it is what God wants us to do when we use our God-given talents for success.

Zach knows that everything he has is by God's grace, and there is no doubt that he has very strong Faith.

I have known Zach for many years, and I can tell you in the many talks we've had that he has his values in order. I will never forget one of the conversations we had when he told me he follows the three F's. He told me he lives by them in this order:

1.    Faith
2.    Family
3.    Friends

On the PGA Tour, he is part of a regular Bible study group. Zach is also very generous in his giving of time, money and teaching. He is the epitome of what we wish all athletes, celebrities, and successful people would be.

As a Christian, we are not supposed to suppress our beliefs and values but let it be known that we give all credit to God for all we have. It does not matter if we are the best golfer in the world or the best security guard at our local mall, God has given us special gifts, talents and blessings, and He deserves the credit. When we fail to give Him credit when given our own pulpit, then we have not passed the test.

God gives us these talents and wants us to give Him the credit because we know these talents are from Him. I thank God every day for everything I have in my life. I am getting better at giving Him credit when I have a pulpit. Some people get it wrong when they hear people give credit to God. They believe that the individual is saying God wanted them to succeed over others.

Zach and others, however, are simply using the pulpit they were given to thank God. Most of the time we hear athletes say their success is due to all their hard work or that they deserve the rewards, and they make it all about themselves. Publicly recognizing Our Father in Heaven is the right thing to do, and all of us should be more like Zach when we achieve success.

As we grow up, we all have people we look up to or idolize. They have a tremendous impact on how we act. If we see an athlete we admire acting poorly, we may think that is how we need to act to become successful.

I have seen a lot of young golfers who idolize Tiger Woods. They all swear out loud when things don't go well, and they tend to be very unhappy individuals during competition. They will throw clubs and act poorly throughout the event because they learned from the guy they watched growing up and believe it is the right way to act.

What do you think would happen if they grew up admiring Zach instead? Wouldn't it be refreshing and possibly have a greater impact on society and generations to follow?

When I saw Tiger act poorly during tournaments, it reinforced my belief that athletes need to act more like Zach. Zach has his priorities in order and knows that his results on the golf course have no bearing on his eternal life. Golf is what he does to provide for his family and is his pulpit for others to see. His reactions are those of a man who knows there is more to life than the golf tournament in which he is playing.

What do you think when you watch someone like Tiger Woods swear and act poorly? What do you think the effect would be if he acted like Zach? Do you think Tiger is appreciative to God for all he has been given? Do you see how we all learn from everything we witness throughout life?

Most of us wish we could play golf like Tiger Woods, act as well as Tom Cruise or win the lottery, but, in truth, if good fortune were to happen to us, would we give credit where credit is due? How do we each envision we would act if all our material dreams came true? If we do have Faith, do we make God proud by expressing our values? Those who know us should know we have a strong

Faith.

God knows us and only gives us what we can handle. I read that the majority of lottery winners and professional athletes from basketball and football end up broke with their lives in shambles. Is it possible they weren't grateful for the riches and weren't good stewards of the gifts God gave them?

You never know when you will be given a pulpit from which to speak, but when it happens are you ready to give God credit? Consider how you would act so that you can pass the test when given the opportunity. As Americans, we are so blessed, yet most of us fail to recognize it and base our worth strictly on what material goods we have right now. Be grateful, and be good stewards of the blessings God has given you.

### ~ Pass the Test ~
How would you handle success? Would you give God credit? In truth we all are very blessed and should give thanks to Our Father in Heaven daily. Good role models like Zach know that everything they have is from God. Be a good role model to those around you.

# Chapter 128

*Oprah Winfrey*

I ONCE SAW an Oprah show where she gave everyone in the audience a significant amount of money. Her crowd went crazy believing it was a generous gift from Oprah as she has been known to do in previous shows. Then the crowd was told that there was a string attached. Those who received the gift from Oprah had to document how they used the money for the benefit of others. The follow-up show was pretty amazing.

Everyone they documented told of how they felt phenomenal from the good they did with the money. Many spoke of how they made the money multiply for even greater use. Some increased the amount by adding their own money to make it a better gift for others. The stories were very heartwarming and many of them cried with joy, including Oprah. It was a great lesson for those who saw or participated in the show.

Oprah has always been a very giving person who is very grateful for what she has earned. She is by all accounts a very good person. Can you imagine what effect she would have on thousands and thousands of people if she were to outwardly express Faith in God through Jesus?

Can you imagine what would have happened if the show had been filled with thanks to God? I pray for Oprah and others who are influential and have huge followings that they will experience and acknowledge God's Love and be willing to express it outwardly.

**~ Pass the Test ~**
Consider demonstrating God's nature by giving financially. See what it does for your heart.

# Chapter 129

## *Stop Expecting Perfect*

WHETHER IT IS politics or following God, too many of us notice others' faults as a way of not engaging in activities or beliefs we know we need to. "It's not fair" seems to be the favorite saying for everything in life. Life was never meant to be perfect nor fair. If it were, none of us would learn anything or believe in anything. Adversity is one way that we form opinions and beliefs.

### Faith versus Lies

When we have full conviction in our Faith in Jesus Christ Our Savior and Lord, we have nothing to be afraid of. When we tell the truth, we have nothing to be afraid of. When we lie, we live in fear, and it will eat away at us. The United States of America has allowed its leaders to lie and distort the truth for so long that it has become acceptable when politicians lie or deviate from the truth. We have become numb to all that happens in Washington, D.C.

Stop it! Demand the truth! It is grim because all the lies have caused problems economically and morally. Don't ever allow the people you elect get away with lying. We all make mistakes, but a true Christian owns their mistakes and corrects them.

Faith is what the USA was established upon, and we must know that our leaders follow Jesus Christ Our Savior and Lord. Everything we are about starts with God and our Faith in Him. The day after 9/11 (the day we were attacked by terrorists), our country banded together and almost everyone turned to God. This is because deep down we recognize our need for God. Because of God, we know the difference between good and bad.

I once heard Glenn Beck talk about fear. He quoted a famous speech of FDR in which he said "we have nothing to fear but fear itself". Glenn said this was poppycock because it makes no sense. What we have to be afraid of is not being prepared. When you have true Faith, you are prepared, and you do not fear death. If you are afraid of death, then you may need to get your Christian life in order.

It is pretty simple, what would you prefer out of our leaders? Those who distort the truth and pit Americans against Americans and who run campaigns based on hatred and negative messages or leaders whose actions back up their Faith? We should never have to question a leader's Christian values. We may not agree with them on all issues, but we should be confident in their Faith.

Stop listening to the press when they lie to us. Quit giving them credit by listening to them. It is up to us to help each other and live life with upright morals and Faith. Do not allow others to create doubt in what we know is right. Follow God, He is always there for all of us.

We all are Loved equally by Him, and He blesses all of us. It is up to us to help those around us in their journey. It is not up to government to take God's place. You can live a life filled with joy no matter what your circumstances if you choose. It is never too late to choose joy. It is never too late for us to turn our lives over to God.

## ~ Pass the Test ~

Support those you believe rather than supporting those who create and further hatred. Use your gifts, talents and blessings to make your life and those lives around you filled with joy.

# Chapter 130

## *Filters*

As we become more selfish as a population, we push our Christian values aside more and more often. It is time to look in the mirror and truthfully answer this question for each decision: Am I doing what I want or what God wants? Be truthful. Unfortunately, the answer for most of our activities results in a selfish answer.

Selfishness becomes easier and easier because we have either blurred the line or completely eliminated the God filter in our lives. To make things worse, our new filter for a lot of what we do is the government. We expect our leaders to answer our questions and needs when, instead, they should be the last option. Even harder to fathom is that our leaders, those who are on TV day after day, are making it okay to eliminate our Christian filter.

They have decided to tell half-truths or just outright lies while taking God out of the picture. As they continue to act with no Christian values, the public has gotten to the point that we believe we can stretch the truth or act selfishly because everyone else is. We need to be a part of this change.

Every one of us should use the Christian grid before we do anything. We need to eliminate bad behavior that we continually allow to happen in the name of freedom. This is not what the United States of America stands for. We are one country under God. Period. We should demand that bad behavior be changed. This needs to start at the individual level and spread from there.

We need to be Christians first — in every instance. We need to stop supporting or allowing bad behavior. Say no to greed, strip clubs, bad television and movies, gambling, impurity and coarse language and become a leader. Begin educating others and help others to stop bad behavior because they choose Jesus.

### ~ Pass the Test ~
Make it a priority to run everything through a Christian filter. When we do this, we will change our lives and can have a positive effect on those around us.

# Chapter 131

## Doing What Is Right Is Easy

WHEN YOU CHOOSE to do things wrong, things get difficult and more complex. Choosing between right and wrong may not always be easy, but through God we can know that choosing right will always be the correct decision. This has become very evident in how our government has worked over the years and especially in the Obama years. Think about how complex our country is now due to all the rules and regulations our overbearing government has enacted.

When government pushes aside God and tries to take His place, our lives become confusing and our lives can become filled with hatred. Think about how you react when you think about our President, Congress and Judges. For so many people, it makes their blood boil. This is because our government has tried to take the place of God.

When you think about Jesus Christ, how do you feel? What would happen, if we all turned our lives over to God? Would our communities, states, and country be better? It is up to each one of us individually to live a Christ-filled life and through these actions help lead others to God. We need to do this with heartfelt Love and Grace (like our Father in Heaven does for us daily).

Only through choosing right over wrong can we lead others to Christ. Yes, we will make mistakes because all of us sin, but Jesus makes it possible to live a life of Faith with the ability to choose right over wrong. Those with Faith will always be forgiven when we ask for it from Our Father in Heaven.

## ~ **Pass the Test** ~
It may not seem like it, but choosing right over wrong is always better and easier in the end. Put God first in your life no matter what.

# Chapter 132

## *Mob Rules*

IT IS ALWAYS easier to go along with a group because we can justify our actions and not be easily singled out. The old adage says that if they are doing it, then I can do it. Unfortunately, this is often not true. Throughout the world in countries like Greece and even in the United States, people are turning to violence and unsavory tactics to make their point when they disagree with one another.

This is not how God-fearing people should act towards others. The ends do not justify the means. We need to Love others and act as God would want us to.

### ~ Pass the Test ~
Always follow God in your actions. Do not let groups of people ever influence your actions in a way that goes against God. Live life with Love and Grace as He does for us.

# Chapter 133

## *Blurring the Lines*

MOST OF US are raised to know the difference between right and wrong. Unfortunately, because life can be difficult, we may try to blur the line between them so we can justify choosing wrong. We might enjoy sports because we are part of the team, celebrities because they are famous, alcohol and drugs because we feel better and because we get to act differently than we know we should. When we participate in drugs or alcohol, we have a built-in excuse as to why we made bad decisions or acted poorly.

When we root for a team, we can act like the rest of the mob with the mentality that if they are doing it then we can as well. When we follow celebrities who get away with a lot, we figure we can as well. In all instances we are looking for a way to act badly.

In politics, we hear the word "compromise" used all the time. The problem with that is that one party can toss out a bunch of really bad ideas because they know the other side will have to agree on some of them in the name of compromise.

There is no compromise between God and the devil. Putting ourselves in positions so that we can make bad decisions is wrong. Life is hard, but that does not give us the right to knowingly position ourselves so we can make bad decisions.

Right is right, and wrong is wrong. God wants to forgive us, but He requires us to repent and turn from that behavior and making that mistake again.

### ~ Pass the Test ~

Always live life with the fear of God. Stay away from situations that encourage or make it easier to make bad decisions.

# Chapter 134

## *Do Not Rely on Anyone Else*

IN OUR COUNTRY we have been told how to live and whom to turn to when things go wrong. It is up to each of us to help each other using the gifts, talents and blessings we have. Each of us will be filled with joy and happiness now and forever if we follow our Christian values. It is up to us to exhibit the Love which Our Father in Heaven shows us.

No matter what happens, when we live life with Faith, Love and Hope we will enjoy eternal happiness. Never forget what you believe and live life to the fullest using your God-given gifts and virtues. How you respond and think about everything around you is the ultimate test. Through Jesus Christ, we are saved and we can all be together in Heaven forever, if each of us follow in Jesus Christ's steps.

Every day we should think about Jesus Christ and the sacrifice He made for us so that we may achieve our goals of obedience to Him.

**~ Pass the Test ~**
Do not rely on others. You can never go wrong by following Jesus Christ Our Savior and Lord.

# Chapter 135

## *Heaven Is a Choice*

OUR FATHER IN Heaven Loves us unconditionally and wants us to admit our sins to Him. It is never too late to change our hearts and actions. Heaven can hold all of us, but it is our choice if we want to be with those we Love throughout eternity. It is also our choice to help as many people as we can to see the light and choose to be with us in Heaven.

There is no downside to changing our ways which will help us find the joy in life which God is so willing to provide. Just like anything else, it is not easy but in the end it is the most rewarding thing any child of God can do. Eternity is forever, so we must decide how we want to spend it and with whom.

**~ Pass the Test ~**
Starting right now, you can make a choice to change your heart so that you can spend eternity in Heaven. The great thing about that change is that it will not only result in a joy filled life on Earth but eternity with Our Creator in Heaven forever!!

# Chapter 13

# Chapter 136

## *Morals*

HOW DO WE learn the difference between right and wrong? The basis to all of society is knowing the answer to this question. God teaches us through the Bible how we are to act and treat everyone. We have an enormous problem today with Godly morals. Our government has blurred the line on so many issues as to what is acceptable and not acceptable, and it has trickled down through our culture. As our nation has turned away from God, our morals have become worse and worse. This is not a coincidence.

A lot of the problems come from parents over the last few decades. Time has become such a precious commodity that most families are now putting activities like sporting events for their kids ahead of going to Church. It always amazes me how much our children are paying attention and learning from what we do and say. If we drive and use a cell phone to text or call people, our kids will grow up to believe that this is what they should do when they drive. If we use foul language when we are upset, our kids will grow to use the same language when they get upset.

If we put your own needs ahead of God, they will do the same. What lessons do our kids learn from us if we only go to Church when it is convenient, or we only occasionally consult God?

While raising our children, we stress many things that

they need to do to grow up and be successful. From hygiene matters to study habits to how to play a sport better to a good work ethic—these life lessons we teach our kids are to help them achieve goals in the near future and beyond. What about eternity? Do we want to spend eternity with our families and friends?

We can be shortsighted in our views and put so much emphasis on personal accomplishments that we lose sight of what is truly important. Teaching our kids about God and helping them grow in their Faith should be our first goal. Raising our children to put Jesus Christ first is the only way to give our families a chance to be together forever.

When my kids were young, I was afraid to fly. I was afraid I wouldn't be around to teach them about life. I wanted to be a part of teaching them to put God first in everything they do. If they are strong in their Faith and try to be the best Christians they can be, I know we will be together forever. I also know they will handle life well and be successful in life because they will have God's values to follow. I don't care if they cut grass for a living or become President the United States, they will know what true joy is all about and make others' lives around them better.

God tells us to put one day aside to worship Him and relax and think about Him. Church is the most important component for me on this day. By putting sporting events or other activities ahead of going to Church, I teach my kids that I only call on God when it is convenient.

When I think of all the things I want to consistently teach my children in hopes they will be happy and better humans, I believe that a place that teaches the real meaning of joyful and everlasting life is a good place to start. No sporting event for a young child is going to bring more happiness or teach them more life skills than as spending time with Christ's Church.

Jesus Christ needs to be our main teaching to our kids. Our morals come from Him through the Bible. Our kids will become better people and learn to handle life's curveballs when they have God as the foundation of their lives.

## ~ Pass the Test ~

Make God the foundation of your life. Make Church the most important priority for your family on Sunday. All of our morals come from the Bible, so we should put it first ahead of all else. If we want to give our families the best probability to be together for eternity, it has to start with putting our Spiritual life ahead of all else.

Eternal life is not a fleeting moment. It should be our number one priority. We will feel like we've done the job God has called us to if we instill God's principles and foundation into our children's lives--into how they think and live out their decisions.

# Chapter 137

## *Past Is Over*

I REALLY ENJOY playing the game of golf. I've learned a lot of lessons as I've played. For the most part it is a self-governing game in which you call penalties on yourself if you have an infraction. I used to be a professional golfer. One of the advantages I had was that I could usually put the past behind me. To be a great golfer you truly need to play one shot at a time and especially not dwell on the past.

Many things are out of your control once the ball is in the air. The golf ball can bounce in any direction, and you have no control. Many times it will be my own fault that I am in a bad situation in the rough or a bunker. I need to learn from the mistake that has resulted in this undesirable outcome.

Sometimes it is "bad luck," and there's nothing I can do about it. I cannot let what has happened affect my next move or it will usually compound the error.

In life, we all make mistakes. It may be a lie we told or a justification we have for our less than good behavior. What is remarkable is that our God is so amazing to show us Grace at all times—even when we don't deserve it.

His Love is unconditional, and all we have to do is repent and turn from making that mistake going forward. Sometimes it feels like we have so many mistakes or sins that we can't overcome them, but God will show any one of his children Grace. God longs to show us Grace when we make the heartfelt request.

### ~ Pass the Test ~

Don't let the past ruin your future. We can change our ways right now if we want a better life. Learn from the past, and turn over your sins to God right now. He Loves us so much that He will help us through anything. Take the step of Faith.

# Chapter 138

## *Only I*

ONLY I HEAR things the way I hear them.
Only I see what I see.
Only I decipher information the way I do.
Only I am where I am at right now.
Only I can teach others the way I teach.
Only I can show my Faith the way I can show it.
Only I have my particular tests each day.
Only I have my brain.
Only I can grow my Faith.
Only I am in charge of my daily activities.
Only I decide what mood I am in.
Only I decide what is important to me.
Only I encounter what I encounter every day.
Only I.................................

### ~ Pass the Test ~

It is up to me how I choose to process life. Anyone can put Jesus Christ first throughout their life.

Anyone can find joy in everything because of God's Love and Grace for every one of us.

Only I can affect my life and those I encounter the way that I can affect them.

# Chapter 139

## *Further the Kingdom*

I PLAY CARDS a few times a month. In that group, one of the regulars has become a nice acquaintance of mine. I have gotten to know him pretty well. He's around 30 years old, and he is nice but unhappy. I can tell his life has no meaning by the way he talks.

For months I have been talking to him about his Faith. God has put him on my heart. I haven't knocked him over the head with it, but I'm aware of his need and am prepared to talk each time we are together.

I have invited him to join me at Church, but he has told me he is not worth saving and that I would probably burn if he went to Church with me. Even though he lives a very sin-filled life, he is worthy of hearing about God's love and forgiveness. Everyone is worth saving. Jesus taught us this over and over and over again.

One night he asked me why I cared. I told him God has put him on my heart because he must be on God's heart. Deep down all of us can tell when someone is in pain by their talk and actions. We know then that it is time to step up and help.

### ~ Pass the Test ~
We come across lost souls often. Like Jesus, we need to show them Love and Grace in an effort to help them find God's love, forgiveness and salvation.

## About the Author

Chris Kramer is a successful entrepreneur, former professional golfer, husband, dad and reluctant author.

Originally this book was something God put on his heart to share with his family. But then as some of his friends and his pastor started to read sections of what he was writing, they encouraged him to get this out to more people.

They let him know that these short observations about God and life were helping them to interject more of their Faith into their daily walk.

As a result, Chris published this first collection of short writings in the hopes of inspiring and equipping others to put God first in real world ways.

## Can you help?

If you liked this book and it was helpful to you, could you PLEASE leave a review on Amazon? Simply visit http://www.amazon.com/dp/ B016B50DIG/ to leave your honest feedback!

Reviews are really important to the success of a book—so if you like (or don't like!) what you've read, PLEASE take 2 minutes to leave your honest review —I really appreciate it.